The Future Consumer

Praise for *The Future Consumer*

A clear and convincing "wake-up" call to an intriguing and fascinating business future. Read it. Heed it!
> —**Lou Pritchett**, *former VP Sales*, **Procter & Gamble (P&G)**

The marketplace is changing faster than our marketers. This book will help our marketers catch up.
> —**Philip Kotler**, *Prof. of Marketing, J. L.Kellogg Graduate School of Management*, **Northwestern University**

Companies with designs on leading their industry during the late 1990s and beyond must refocus to compete. This "glocal" marketing model, with its relevant examples and checklists, provides an insightful yet simple way to make the shift.
> —**Ross Roberts**, *VP/GM, Ford Division*, **Ford Motor Company**

Thought provoking and challenging, Feather describes a consumer who will require many companies to change their way of business. Those that change will grow and prosper; those that fail to change may disappear.
> —**Alfred Lynch**, *President & CEO*, **JCPenney International Incorporated**

To plan effective marketing programs and succeed in the 21st century, managers must read *THE FUTURE CONSUMER* — now!
> —**Daniel McGee**, *Chairman/CEO*, **American Motion Systems**

A comprehensive "must read," Frank Feather elevates your thinking, challenging you to provide the thought leadership any business needs if it is to grow in the late 1990s.
> —**Dennis Frezzo**, *President*, **KFC Canada**

A powerful business blueprint. With insight and enthusiasm, Frank Feather uses one example after another to synthesize market trends into a realistic strategic framework.
> —**Joel Alper**, *President*, **COMSAT Systems**

Do you know who your customers are? With clarity and insight, this book presents strategies to attract and retain them for decades!
> —**Jack Shand**, *President*, **Canadian Society of Association Executives**

A fascinating, fun-to-read review of changing consumer behavior and how smart firms are adapting to meet cultural and lifestyle needs.
> —**Charlotte Cuff**, *Director-Public Affairs*, **American Cyanamid**

Explains the new competencies that companies need if they are to succeed in tomorrow's marketplace.
> —**Norma Cooper**, *Vice-President*, **Canadian Reinsurance Company**

A jewel box that sparkles brilliantly with million-dollar ideas.
> —**Angela Cocomile**, *Investment Advisor*, **Nesbitt Thomson**

The era of serving the specific and exact needs of the individual is upon us. To prosper, selling organizations must change their "modus operandi." Frank Feather sounds the alarm; we must listen.
> —**Bob Brema**, *President*, **William M. Dunne & Associates Limited**

The business dynamics of today and tomorrow are very different from those of the 1970s and 1980s. *THE FUTURE CONSUMER* provides excellent insight into those changes and the new skills required for companies to succeed in a "glocal" economy.
> —**Steve Dengate**, *President*, **Anixter Canada Incorporated**

Excellence is a key ingredient of customer service and this book serves up enough inspiring recipes to let you mix your own success.
> —**John Geci**, *President & CEO*, **Canadian Council of Grocery Distributors**

An entertaining and challenging book which I recommend to all executives faced with current-day problems.
> —**Janice Scites**, *President*, **Connecticut Mutual Customer Services**

The Future Consumer

FRANK FEATHER

Warwick Publishing
Toronto Los Angeles

The Future Consumer
Copyright © 1997 by Frank Feather and Glocal Marketing Inc

Published by the Warwick Publishing Group:
24 Mercer Street, Suite 300, Toronto, Canada M5V 1H3; and
1424 North Highland Avenue, Los Angeles, CA 90027.

Cover Design: Diane Farenick
Layout: Kimberley Davison
Author Photograph: Ian Davenport Photographic Services Inc.
Editorial Services: Harry Endrulat

ISBN 1-895629-81-0

Distributed in the United States and Canada by:
Firefly Books Ltd., 3680 Victoria Park Avenue, Willowdale, Canada M2H 3K1.

This publication is designed to provide accurate and authoritative information in regard to the subject matter covered. While a great deal of care has been taken to provide accurate and current information, the ideas, suggestions, and conclusions presented in this book are subject to various laws. It is sold on the understanding that the author and publisher are not engaged in rendering legal or accounting advice, which should be sought from professionals in those fields.

GLOCAL™ is a registered trademark of Glocal Marketing Inc.:
 3511 Silverside Road, Suite 105, Wilmington, DE 19810; and
 P.O.Box 38, Aurora, Ontario, Canada L4G 3H1 (Tel: 905/642-9090)

Printed and Bound in Canada

Contents

THE FUTURE CONSUMER:
Shopping in 2004

Imagine a brand-new future when shopping will *always* be a joyful and deeply satisfying personal experience.

Welcome to the year 2004. It's true: A marketing revolution which began in the mid-1990s has changed *everything* in favor of *you*, the customer. High-touch service and gee-whiz computers made it all possible. There's no more hard-sell hype, junk mail, or telemarketing. And you're treated as an honored guest no matter where or how you shop.

While visiting a store is a joy, half the time you buy from the comfort of your virtual-reality media room at home. You only visit a store after scanning a computerized global product catalog and electronically "browsing" the store with an amazing *TeleCom Wallet*.

Magical Wizardry of "TeleCom Wallets"

The *TeleCom Wallet (TW)* of 2004 is quite something. As it developed during the late 1990s, the *TW* replaced all the stuff we used to carry in a wallet or purse. No more cash, cash dispenser cards, credit cards, debit cards, checks, telephone calling cards, health insurance cards, house keys, car keys, driving licenses, transit tickets or tokens — all everyday transaction needs are handled by your *TW*. It has replaced your passport, birth certificate, marriage certificate, and social insurance card.

Today, your *TW* carries full data about you and each member of your household, your possessions, and all your product and service preferences. It even stores virtual reality images of every room in your home and all the clothes in your wardrobe. And, yes, it even files your tax return.

By comparison, the *TWs* of the early 1990s were primitive, awkward, computer-like gizmos. These museum pieces even had clumsy names: "personal digital assistants" (PDAs), "information appliances," "pocket organizers," or "palm-tops." Typical of a fast-developing technology, the manufacturers didn't know what to call them. And, as smart as they were, there was no built-in telephone.

For example, the **Sharp** *Wizard* "organizer" had a full keyboard, touch-sensitive screen, and as much power as **Apple**'s first computer. It stored phone numbers, appointments, and memos. But you needed slot-in software cards to send/receive files and faxes or connect with on-line bulletin boards. To make a simple phone call you needed a separate phone.

The **Apple** *Newton* "pen computer" combined a calendar, electronic fax, pager, and computer. It could crudely translate some handwriting into type and could beam information to and from other computers by infrared. Slot-in cards provided city maps, *Fortune 500* company sales/profits data, crosswords, customized news clips, and E-mail linkage. **AT&T**'s *EO* was similar, as was the much better **Hewlett-Packard** *HP-100LX*.

But all these clever devices had a big shortcoming. Back then, cellphone components interfered with computers, so manufacturers couldn't combine the two functions into the single-unit *TW* tele-computer people really wanted. Instead, you got wireless slot-in cards that linked up with a separate cellphone, making the full set of equipment just too cumbersome for most people to use.

Single-unit *TWs* finally evolved along with the convergence of computer, phone, satellite, and virtual reality technology.

First, in 1994, the **General Magic** global alliance of **AT&T-Apple-Motorola-Sony-Matsushita-Phillips** came out with *Magic Cap* and *Telescript* (the first PDA operating system software and programming language) that let PDAs, PCs, and TVs communicate with each other. Within a year, **General Magic** was selling the first true *TW*, **Microsoft** came out with a *Winpad* version, **Motorola**'s *Envoy* had a built-in modem, and **AT&T** launched *Sage*, the first-ever phone-computer combo.

Those 1994 gizmos could access weather, news, and stockmarket reports. You could also use them to order *concierge* services such as flower, gift, and theater ticket delivery. As well, **Ford** and **GM** began to introduce dashboard electronic maps and route-planning for car drivers. Touchscreens let you reserve a motel room, book a flight, or find the nearest fast-food outlet.

Parallel to these advances, strides were made in telephone technology itself. **Matsushita**'s *Panasonic* introduced a wristwatch-sized, flip-open, cordless phone. It had a mini-keypad, quick-dial number memory, redial, built-in intercom, and a voice scrambler for privacy. **Casio** also announced the world's first universal remote control wristwatch combo that operated your VCR, TV, and cable box — and told the time. By 1997, these features were so commonplace that, in 2001, the Gore administration started giving every new kindergarten kid a free wristwatch *TW* with a single phone number they'll keep for life, no matter where in the world they live.

Thanks to satellite technology, **Motorola**'s *Iridium* system created a global cellular phone network in 1997, bringing worldwide TV access, no matter where you are. Today's *TW* is great for travellers. It has a locating device that tells you exactly where you are on the globe, automatically translates to/from foreign languages as you converse, and can recognize handwriting in any major language.

Early satellites let **Singapore Airlines** introduce the first onboard "skyphone" and later the first inflight "skyfax" service. **American Airlines** installed digital phones on planes in 1994 so that passengers with PCs could send/receive faxes and communicate with other computers on the ground. **Boeing**'s very first *777* had fold-down tele-computers in the back of every seat and those in its upcoming *2007 SpacePlane* will have virtual reality.

In about 1998, *TWs* themselves got virtual reality, originally a 1980s technology spun off from flight simulators used to train airforce pilots. Virtual reality gives you the impression of being immersed in a 3-D image. In the 1996 version, you wore a bulky headset connected to a tele-computer and used an electrically-wired glove to manipulate what you saw. The latest version, which came out in 2001, is wireless and has no glove. It looks no different than a pair of eyeglasses. You change the image by spoken commands, eye movements, and hand gestures via a tiny camera on your multimedia set.

Just as *Star Trek*'s "transporter" let Scotty "beam" people from place to place, your *TW* lets you "visit" libraries, museums, data bases, catalogs, malls, and stores from home or anyplace else. Since 2003, you can talk back and forth with family, friends, coworkers, or sales consultants through your *TW* screen. You can also tele-commute to **Time-Warner**'s data-base schools and the **Apple-Xerox TeleUniversity** or convert reams of **McGraw-Reuters**' planet-wide data to your personal needs.

Some 55 million first-generation *TWs* were in use in North America by the year 2000. Today, more than 160 million people use full-blown *TWs* for their everyday needs.

Life's a breeze!

○ ○ ○

Here's how it all works — for tele-banking, buying cars, scheduling infotainment, ordering fast food, and tele-shopping from home or shopping in person from stores and supermarkets.

Tele-Finance

The *TW* tracks your money and pays your bills. It *is* your bank account! This electronic money revolution totally transformed banking. Banks always were in the information *about* money business, but few realized it until **AT&T**, which issued a credit card way back in 1989, merged with **Citibank** in 1997 and shook the entire finance industry.

TWs forced changes to all kinds of money cards. First, the banks combined the features of "credit" cards with Japanese "prepaid" cards. Prepaid cards were paid for in advance and used to buy everything from transit tokens to major household goods. As you used it, the card's balance declined and, like your electric car's battery, had to be regularly recharged.

Meanwhile, after the 1989-92 "Mini-Depression," most North Americans switched from borrowing to saving, from credit cards to debit cards. Debit cards were like the old automated teller cards. A paperless check, they were credit cards without the credit, with payments taken straight from your bank account. In the new savings-oriented economy, **Visa's** *Check Card* was as popular as its ordinary credit card by 1998.

Today, the credit, debit, and prepaid features are combined in your *TW* **AT&T-Citibank** electronic account. Your balance floats: A positive balance earns interest and a 5% "purchase perk" of electronic coupons; an overdraft is charged interest and a 5% commission.

With all bills paid by your *TW*, cash became a rarity and all automated teller machines (ATMs) were replaced by electronic transaction kiosks (ETKs) by 1998. Today there are few checks or credit card chits to clear, and banks are full financial service firms. Because your *TW* has built-in money payment features, you can bank from home or anywhere you happen to be.

As far back as 1994, **EON** developed a system that let you manage your personal financial affairs through a TV set using **Intuit**'s popular *Quicken* software. The same year **Citibank** began aggressively marketing tele-banking through an advanced phone made by **Phillips**. An early form of *TW*, the phone had a fold-away digital display screen and slide-away typewriter-like keyboard. You could choose from a menu of banking, bill payment, stock trading, phone directories, and voice mail. Shopping and airline reservation services were added in 1997.

Sanwa Bank developed an expert computer system called *Best Mix* that customized investment portfolios to your individual needs. With this system, Japanese bank officers made house calls, and by 1996, all our banks were doing it. Using your ITV (interactive TV) as a computer terminal, the bank officer keyed in data about your personal financial situation and goals. Instead of taking hours to produce an ideal global portfolio, *Best Mix* took only five minutes. It figured in global tax rates, interest rates, and yields on every type of investment.

The bank officer ran various simulations, covering different investment options and risk factors. Once you settled on a preferred mix, she immediately sent buy and sell orders over your ITV unit. Now, of course, you can do all that for yourself. **AT&T-Citibank** licensed the *Best Mix* service and added it to their *TW* tele-banking package.

They also added virtual reality so you can "fly over" your global investment portfolio in 3-D depth. Just like hovering over Manhattan in a helicopter, your various investments stand out like skyscrapers as their clustered bar-charted values rise and fall with the nonstop global market.

Your *TW* constantly updates your portfolio and presents you with new, custom-tailored investment options 24 hours a day, keeping track of all your financial affairs.

Tele-Buying a Car
You can even buy a car, of your precise choice, from home. Until the mid-1990s,

you'll remember, most of the auto industry was still product driven. How could you forget?!

Many firms tried to ram cars down your throat so the factory could maintain steady output. Most dealerships were horse-trading arenas, with the salesman (95% were male) trying to outwit you on price — something we all thoroughly detested.

And, being a "seller" rather than a product specialist, he often didn't know enough about the product. Instead of educating you about a car's features and the benefits of ownership, he was trained to close the deal. After some intense haggling, usually not with him but with a mysterious sales manager you never met, the deal was signed.

There was little genuine interest in what you needed or wanted. Rather than getting a car with chosen options, too often you had to take one that had sat on the lot for two months — and which always fell short of expectations. Three months later, if you were lucky, you got a computerized thankyou letter from the manufacturer. Then they basically forgot about you, expecting you to come back in three years.

It's no wonder that lots of people switched to Japanese cars. And the reasons went way beyond quality. In 1997, **Toyota** introduced its Japanese-style network of dealers, each selling specific types of car, to North America. Whichever outlet you dealt with, they treated you as an "owner" (not a customer) and welcomed you as a "member of the Toyota family."

Even back then, most of **Toyota**'s associate sales agents were college grads with intensive courses in product information, order taking, financing, insurance, and owner relationship building. Today, they all graduate from the **GM-Toyota Tele-University**. Working in teams, they know all about the business and understand how to treat you.

In 1997, they also began selling cars by personal house call, as they had in Japan since the 1980s. The team of agents keeps biographical profiles of every local household and makes appointments to visit both existing and prospective owners. During the visit, your household profile is updated from your *TW* for the number and ages of people, types of existing cars, and their expected time of replacement.

The sales associate suggests the best new vehicle to specifically meet your family's changing needs. You can "test drive" it using your virtual reality eyeglasses and a steering hookup the agent brings with her. (Yes, 60% of today's car agents are women.)

If you like the car, she offers to bring a similar demo vehicle that you keep for a week. Whatever model you finally buy, it is made to your precise order; there's no dickering over options or price. She zaps your order straight to the factory and, within three days, personally brings the car to your home.

Many people buy cars from home using a PC. In 1993, **GM** began treating potential buyers to a round of golf at the *Buick Open* course at Warwick Hills Country

Club in Grand Blanc, Michigan — via computer disk. The 1996 disk went to 650,000 people who asked for it. Containing two sections — a golf video game and product info about *Buick* cars — the disk had color videos and data for each model, including price, fuel economy, and vehicle features. You could select the features you wanted (two doors, price range, or whatever), and the interactive disk then offered all models with those features for closer study. The animated disk showed the chosen car being built, and you could interact with it and take it for a "test drive."

Other people buy cars through ITV shopping. In 1994, **GM** began offering *Pontiac* on **Home Shopping Network**'s *TV Car Showroom* program. The program set resembled a car showroom, displaying *Grand Am* and other *Pontiac* models. Hosted by famous racecar drivers, the program showed video clips of the cars and again you could switch to virtual reality mode, link your *TW* to the ITV program, and take the car for a spin. You could also get more-detailed model info downloaded to your *TW*. The *TV Car Showroom* program became today's full auto industry shopping channel in 1997.

If you prefer, of course, you can still go to a dealer or auto supermarket to buy in person. And you'll be in for a pleasant surprise. Today's agents are paid on a group commission basis. So they no longer lunge at you like sharks in a feeding frenzy when you first walk in.

Instead, a hostess greets you and escorts you to an elaborate but welcoming computer display in the owner's lounge. And, again, since your *TW* contains all your household info and car ownership data, you plug it into the display to update the car retailer's computer. The interactive multimedia system then presents new models to suit your family's needs, including current prices.

Again, you can take a virtual reality "test drive" of any model which takes your fancy. A sample of each car is also displayed in the adjacent showroom for you to explore. The sales team waits patiently for you to approach them with specific questions, whereupon everyone joins in a group discussion. They really try to educate you about the product. Although I'm sure they are obsessed with market share, they are concerned about *your* needs, not those of the factory. They genuinely want to build owner relationships. Lastly, you're invited to take home a demo for a week or so. One of the associates will deliver it for you within the hour.

Some 70% of cars are still sold by dealers or auto supermarkets; the rest are sold during house calls or through tele-shopping methods. Whichever way you buy, after your car is delivered you get periodic courtesy calls from your personal sales associate. To stay close, she sends birthday and graduation cards. She'll also call when the children are about to enter college (or graduate and start a career) to ask if they need a car.

How do they do it? The elaborate data collection on your preferences is fed constantly and systematically to new product development teams. This links you to the research lab and factory, and they adjust designs and flex the assembly line to meet *your* needs. The entire distribution chain of a leading car maker like **Toyota** contains only five days' supply, 95% of them preorders. Retailers carry only showroom and demo models.

Most dealers simply weren't info-intensive enough to compete. In the early 1990s, a typical dealer carried two months' inventory, and there was poor coordination between dealers and the car maker's sales divisions and product planners. Only **GM**'s **Saturn** adopted the streamlined Japanese approach.

Many dealers were displaced by **Ford-Sears Automart** which became the biggest auto supermarket. They carry every make, including those of the three remaining dedicated dealer chains, **GM**, **Saturn**, and **Toyota**. Most cars are not even made by the car design firms but by **Magna**, which is promising overnight customized assembly by 2010.

That's not all. Cars are guaranteed for 20 years and 30% of them are electric- or methanol-powered. **GM**'s electric *Impact 2000* was a big seller in the late 1990s, and the new **Ford** *Synthesis 2010* is so much fun to drive.

After the UN Earth Summit and the election of Bill Clinton in 1992, ecology became a top priority. All firms — not just car companies — adopted a "green" ethic. Those that didn't were either legislated out of business or deserted by fleeing customers. People simply demanded products that were earth-friendly *and* fun to use.

Individualized Infotainment

Speaking of fun, everybody tailor-makes their own entertainment these days. There are no more regularly scheduled radio or TV programs; no more reruns. We no longer buy printed books, newspapers, or magazines. Recorded music and videos are obsolete. Just as magazines "demassified" to serve splintering readership groups in the 1980s, since 1998 infotainment mass media can be tailored to the specific interests of single individuals. They call it "mass customization."

In publishing, the former **McGraw-Hill** used to have product divisions cranking out books, magazines, and data banks full of general information. In the mid-1990s, the company created market-focused multimedia groups, each tracking a specific area of interest, such as healthcare or travel. Teams of editors and researchers identified the information needs of each market and created interactive data bases for people to access.

Interactive CDs began to replace encyclopedias in 1992 and books in 1996. To preserve trees, all print media went electronic in 1999. Today's kids don't deliver newspapers; they customize news for people, capturing from the new **McGraw-Reuters** data base precisely what you want to "read" on your *TW*. Old print media like **Time Warner**'s *Time*, *Fortune*, and *Money* magazines and major newspapers became TV channels.

Book publishers either went electronic or shut down. The local library-book-store combo carries only antique and leather-bound collectors' items. You now "browse" a data base for research material. Of course, if you don't want to study it on your *TW* screen, you can print out a paper version in whatever type size or style you prefer. Blind people can print it in braille or hear it in audio.

The only "live" radio or TV broadcasts are urgent news and weather. You don't even tune in for those because **NABC** (the last North American network) downloads urgent news to your multimedia tele-computer. When that occurs, your *TW* flashes a red light, just like the "message waiting" light on those old-fashioned hotel phones. Remember?

Instead, each family member custom-tailors their own radio, TV, and music from **NABC**'s global infotainment file. This all started in 1993 with *The Box*, an interactive pay-per-view TV service operated by **Video Jukebox Network.** In those days, teenagers dialed a 900-number and a three-digit code to select their favorite music videos. Today, they use a *TW* to preselect programs that **NABC** downloads for later viewing.

You select programs with your *TW* much as you once picked books from a library, or videos from a rental store. You can store programs on **Kodak**'s interactive CDVs (videotapes are obsolete) and watch them at a more convenient time. Movies, political debates, and game shows also come over ITV or on interactive CDVs. You can change plot endings and take part in the debates, talk shows, and games. **Matsushita**'s *Panasonic REAL 3DO Interactive Multiplayer* was a breakthrough in consumer electronics. Supported by many software firms, the *3DO* let you play video games on game-maker **Sega**'s full-color, virtual reality, stereo headset in a 360° 3-D world.

In 1994, **Time Warner** first tested its *Full Service Network* in Florida. Viewers could customize their TV schedules, calling up movies, sports, or home shopping at the touch of a button. They could call up individualized horoscopes, financial market info, sports highlights of their favorite teams, or they could browse electronic classified ads. By 1998, kids could play video games against their "telepals" across the globe. Movie buffs could fast-forward, pause, or rewind movie selections at the touch of a button on their *TW*. **GM**, **Ford**, **Chrysler**, and **Nissan** created yet another *Auto Mall* where you could compare cars, watch video "brochures," and set up "test drives" via your *TW*.

Apple's interactive *EZ-TV* had large on-screen icons controlled via remote control. It displayed 12 channels around the screen, with the main viewing channel in the center. For pay-per-view movies, the screen had icons for preview, movie info, and ticket. A click on the ticket icon started an animation where the ticket tore in half, and you were told when the movie would start. **Zing**, an ITV venture of **TCI-Comcast-Turner**, let viewers play along with game shows and sporting events and participate in polls. A personal *ZingDialer* (a crude *TW*, one for each household member) at least eliminated phone interaction with the system. It communicated over cable TV via a set-top *ZingBlaster* which responded to each *ZingDialer* in the room. You could register a score, give an opinion, or buy something. Of course, by 1998, your *TW* did all that.

In 1994, **Hughes** (part of **GM**) began beaming 500 channels of infotainment over *DirecTv* to a small 18-inch satellite dish mounted on your window sill. Initially, people thought having so many channels was ridiculous. They didn't realize that your *TW* would come to "know" you by the program choices you made. Your *TW* constantly offers new material that matches your interests, culling it from all available offerings. In the 500-channel world, a channel is not so much a frequency band as a customized set of infotainment categories. With a *TW*, you make your own channel. When you pick a movie, your *TW*'s "remote" even switches on the popcorn maker in your kitchen.

Ordering Fast Food

Yes, of course you can still order fast food from home. Instead of the telephone, you use your *TW* which zaps through your custom order and requests special delivery on the neighborhood electric car shuttle. Operated in every town and city by **Federal Express**, the world's [#]1 courier/taxi firm, a *FedEx Shuttle* passes your door every 10 minutes. It has an onboard oven and fridge to keep foods hot or cold and brings parcels, groceries, and laundry. And you can hitch a ride from your front door to almost anyplace you want to go. Seniors and teens love it!

The old fast-food chains themselves, responding to multicultural America, have become full menu "glocal" (global + local) delis. **McDonald's** has grown to 50,000 outlets worldwide and, with a diverse menu of global foods to reflect the new multicultural make-up of society, has revived its *"Different tastes for different tastes"* slogan in 1996.

You can eat inside or drive through, ordering your own customized choices from your *TW* in your car just before you arrive or at a bank of touchscreen menu kiosks inside. Yes, all the "Mac Jobs" have disappeared. The order counter has gone and all the hamburgers are flipped by robots these days. In fact, much fast food is made at central kitchens which serve a cluster of outlets and is delivered just in time for your order.

Today's successful fast-food delis such as **McDonald's** and its main rival, **PepsiDeli**, use a blend of global corporate leverage and local entrepreneurial marketing to achieve market dominance. In the late 1990s they broadened their global scope by opening small local scale outlets everywhere.

Tele-Shopping

Retail stores also had to change. Until the late 1990s, they only carried products for which there was enough local demand. But 21st-century retailers offer a global array of products, regardless of local demand. They call it "glocal" marketing, a novel idea which makes it as easy to shop with retailers across the world as it is to shop with retailers half a mile from home.

Electronic advances have brought a world of products into your home. Oh, it's much more exciting than that boring old way of TV shopping, and tele-sales have skyrocketed. In 1992, sales over the **Home Shopping Network** were a mere $5 billion, and only 10% of cable TV subscribers bought anything that way. *Prodigy*, the computer-based venture of **Sears** and **IBM**, had only two million members in 1993. Today, you control the type and sequence of items presented with your *TW*.

After **QVC** (meaning "quality, value, convenience") took over **Home Shopping Network** in 1994 and joined with **Wal-Mart** and **Procter & Gamble** to sell *via* ITV, more than 370 million households worldwide now spend $150 billion a year this way. *Q2*, a second channel, covers entertaining, cooking, gardening, travel, home decor, and exercise. Chatty Joan Rivers even quit talk shows to launch a syndicated show *Can We Shop?* to sell (if you can believe) "exercise jewelry."

QVC spread to the UK, Ireland, and the rest of Europe in an alliance with Britain's **Sky TV**. Another deal with **Grupo TV** broadcasts to Mexico, Spain, Portugal, and Latin America in Spanish and Portuguese. Japan went on the air in 1997 and China in 2002.

Japanese, Chinese, and Europeans also buy from the rival **Universal TeleStores** — a global venture of **Mitsukoshi-Marks & Spencer-JCPenney-AT&T/Citibank**. Picking from 10,000+ services, 310 million households are members of the **Universal TeleStores** family, all using a *TW* to shop from home.

Catalogs also went electronic. They first began using videos because they were good at showing fashions, computers, or intricate insurance policies. But VCRs were too rigid: You could only forward, reverse, or freeze the picture. As mentioned, they became obsolete and were replaced by interactive CDVs (ICDVs) in 1996. The random access feature of ICDVs let you go directly to the portion of the presentation which interested you.

After years of tests, **Apple** finally launched a CD-ROM shopping service in 1996 called *En Passant*, issuing a disk-full of catalogs such as **Lands' End** and **L.L.Bean** clothing, **Tiffany** jewelry, **Pottery Barn** kitchen items, and **Nature Company** products. You could compare competing products side-by-side, browsing by catalog or category-related goods across catalogs. You could make sweaters change color by clicking on color swatches or find the right tie-and-shirt combo. An electronic "valet" let you custom-design a personalized multi-vendor catalog containing only those categories of goods that you cared about.

Today, remember, all that personal preference info is on your *TW*. In fact, because TV-, computer-, and catalog-shoppers were so similar, these businesses all converted to ITV which most people like much better. So did the companies. **Bean**, for example, used to mail out 130 million catalogs a year. To eliminate costly (and taboo) paper, ink, and postage, it fully converted to a multimedia format in 1998.

Until proper *TWs* came out, people also used PCs to shop from home. **CUC**, one of the biggest just-in-time (JIT) electronic retailers, offered discount prices — by computer or phone — on 250,000 brand-name products. **CUC** simply transferred orders to the manufacturer who shipped the product direct by **FedEx** or **UPS**, eliminating stores, parking lots, inventory, insurance, and salespeople. **PC Flowers** began selling blooms on **Prodigy** and other computer shopping systems in 1993. By 1996, it was #1 in sales in the entire **FTD** florist network, grossing $40 million a year, as much as 200 of the old-fashioned florist shops.

Apple's *EZ-TV* also brought virtual reality to retailing. In a virtual mall, you can "walk around" by moving an arrow in the desired direction. You can go into a hat shop, click on a hat on the wall, lift it down, and rotate it — much like viewing it through a video camera. As you buy things, your *TW* keeps tally. Since 1998, young women have shopped for clothes — even their bridal gown — using virtual reality. A TV-type screen shows a selection of gowns and an image of the bride-to-be modeling each one. She can switch gowns and change the length or shape of any gown by voice command.

Since *TWs* became commonplace in 2001, almost everybody does some form of electronic shopping. Before ever going to a store, you electronically preview its contents by donning the virtual reality eyeglasses which connect to your *TW* by wireless infrared transmission. You can preview any product, electronically "cruising" any store to "pick up" items and compare price and label info before deciding what to buy from which store. You may also choose to preorder and have products readied for drive-by pickup in 15 minutes, or have them delivered within an hour.

As shoppers learned they could tele-shop for a trusted product at a competitive price with a guarantee, they also learned that for most products there was no reason for them to waste time in shopping malls.

Mega-Center Malls

Yes, you still go out for what we now call "walkabout" shopping. Some local "shopping malls" still exist but they've changed dramatically since the mid-1990s. There used to be many regional malls, but during the last decade, a third of them merged into mega-centers near major cities. The first, **Triple Five**'s *West Edmonton Mall*, opened in 1989. The next, *Mall of America*, opened near Minneapolis-St. Paul in 1992. Atlanta got one in 1996 in time for the Olympics, quickly followed by SeaTac-Vancouver (1998), Toronto (2000), and Dallas-Ft. Worth (2002). Most big metros are planning one.

The mega-center is a giant gathering place for today's multicultural society — 40% of North Americans are nonwhite — and the stores cater to this *Global*

Village in microcosm. There are multilingual signs, a variety of ethnic outlets, and stores from every part of the world. But it offers more than global shops. It's a climate-controlled, 24-hours-a-day, 365-days-a-year info-shopping and entertainment center with three separate wings.

- The **"carnival wing"** has a game arcade, gambling salon, amusement park, a mini golf course, zoological garden, water slide, swimming pool, wave pool, and indoor beach.
- The **"culture wing"** has about 100 eating places, several night clubs, a concert hall, a live theater, a few movie houses, a dozen virtual reality theaters, an art and rare book gallery, and an ecumenical spiritual center with churches, synagogues, mosques, and temples.
- The **"education wing"** has seminar/teleconference rooms, a vocational school, a tele-learning tutorial center, and a tele-library and E-mail hub.

These services are for those who prefer the thrill of real-life experiences and the 30% of the population which doesn't yet have a virtual reality multimedia room at home.

The mall is also full of interactive computer kiosks equipped with touchscreens and simple menus. Since the 1990s, **Photo Lab** has used kiosks to receive film for processing and sell new film and other photo supplies. **Allstate** has sold insurance at kiosks in department stores and supermarkets, printing out the policy on the spot. At **Hallmark Cards** and **American Greetings** kiosks you can design and print your own greeting cards in minutes. **Personics** kiosks sell gift-pack CDs which you compile from 65,000 available titles. **Florsheim** sells customized shoes via an *Express Stop* kiosk which measures your feet for a precise fit. You specify the color and style you want and the customized shoes are delivered in two days by **UPS**.

Today, there are four million kiosks, making them twice as common as **GE-TeXXon** electric car charging kiosks. The kiosks are everywhere: in the supermarket, auto-mart, department store, individual stores, and fast-food delis.

There are about 500 stores in a mega-center, but many of the old names have vanished. By the late 1980s, there were too many malls, far too many copycat stores, and there was too much merchandise sameness. Again, mediocre retailers and malls went out of business in the "Mini-Depression" of 1989-92. Survivors revamped their operations and switched to "glocal" marketing. This really let them take advantage of the fabulous economic "Super-Boom" which took off in 1994 and is still on a roll.

They were joined by new retailers. Today's popular names include many innovative upstarts from the 1990s. **Brady's Instant Tailor** customizes garments for each member of the family using a 3-D measuring system. **Ben & Jerry's** ice cream lets you customize you own cone from 300+ flavor combos. **Rosenbluth Travel** conducts virtual-reality vacations every half hour. The **Sony-Microsoft Gallery** and **Kodak-Toshiba MediaLab** show off their latest multimedia room technology.

The latest mega-centers also have other innovations such as a **Four Seasons/Marriott** hotel/convention facility, a **McDonald's** *Kidicare Center*, an **Extendicare** retirement condo, and a **Mayo Clinic** mini-hospital and out-patient facility.

Electronic Store-Browsing

Unless you do so from your home or car first, you can use your *TW* to elec-tronically "browse" any store in person. This is due to *Rapid* tags (for *radio-auto product ID*) which replaced bar codes on products in 1996. The tags contain microchips and can be read by various detection devices to speed product han-dling and tracking.

As you walk through a store, reading specific product info into your *TW*, you can compare that info against your personal preferences and against other glob-al products in an evaluation data base. It gives you a product's specs and rates its ease of use, sophistication, quality, and "green" rating.

As in **Toyota** or **Saturn** showrooms, you browse without anyone bugging you to buy. Sales pitches and hype, whether in ads or at the time and place of pur-chase, became counter-productive in the 1990s. Shoppers simply forced sellers to provide info to help them buy knowledgeably and on their terms.

Mass advertising gave way to pay-for-view "info-ads." You select them to learn about products and to comparison shop. So the new focus of selling is *not* to "close the sale" and write out the order. Stores genuinely strive to "serve" you and make sure your expectations are met and exceeded. They really care.

The Body Shop, for example, deliberately does *not* train its people how to "sell." It never has. Rather, it focuses on improving employee knowledge so they can talk enthusiastically to you about products. Like **Toyota**, it long ago showed other merchandisers that, in the end, marketing is not about selling. It is about customers buying. There's no "selling" in stores anymore. The associates are all customer consultants. They "listen" intently to learn about your needs — and then educate you about the product.

Instead of using generalists to "sell" all types of products, shops use specialists to educate you about specific product attributes. They focus on your unique needs and are especially sensitive to your culture.

To better serve African-Americans, for instance, **JCPenney** opened *Authentic African* boutiques in all its stores starting in 1992. They feature fashionable clothing, handbags, hats, and other accessories imported from Africa. The styles are distinct, yet don't look out of place in today's multicultural society. Even folks who are not African-American are wearing them.

These boutiques were so successful that in 1996 **JCPenney** began opening

Authentic Asian and *Authentic Latino* variations. Today, the store is a vibrant kaleidoscope — a true *Global Village* shopping and cultural experience.

Successful department stores retrofit their monoliths back into "departments" — entrepreneurial specialty boutiques run independently within a customer-oriented ambience. **JCPenney** is still one of the majors because it restructured early. As Alfred Lynch, then president and CEO of **JCPenney International**, forecast way back in 1992:

> We'll be a "boundaryless" company, geared exclusively to serve our customers. We won't have "catalog" and "retail" divisions, nor district offices and store management hierarchies. We'll serve customers "seamlessly," regardless of whether they shop in the store or by phone, TV, or computer.

Most department stores persisted in using central buyers, ordering stuff six months in advance from diverse suppliers. Their demise was inevitable when they didn't invest heavily in info-systems that capture the order "flow" in real time.

Leading merchandisers such as **JCPenney**, **Wal-Mart**, **Levi Strauss**, **Benetton**, **The Limited**, and **Gap** simply outflanked other retailers by becoming info-networked companies. They know every day (nay, every second!) how many units of which items are sold in each store, worldwide. Tracking sales in real time, they get instant market research and always have fresh-looking merchandise.

Benetton was first to master this art of *consumer draw* marketing, making just what people want to buy. It always stocked only undyed (that is, white) clothing items, warehousing them at global dyeing nodes. Based on info about each size/color sold in the stores, new merchandise is dyed and shipped, refilling store shelves within three days of its sale.

With their real-time merchandising systems, such retailers brand timeless values such as color and excitement, without losing "in" fashion status. A decade ago, **Benetton**'s founder, Luciano Benetton, explained the chain's popularity this way:

> Each store's product mix simply fits the tastes of its neighborhood, street, or avenue.

For its part, **Wal-Mart** always refused to deal with suppliers who couldn't communicate with it electronically. In effect, ever since 1989, **Wal-Mart**'s checkout registers have been connected to the warehouses of major suppliers like **P&G**, triggering new shipments. By 1995, **K Mart** was doing the same. Both companies' stores each have a satellite dish, keeping HQ fully in tune with the pulse of local markets.

Before *Rapid* tags came along, **Levi Strauss** was swiftly handling products with its *Levilink* system. This electronic buying system slashed reorder time. Barcoded cartons and packing slips hastened shipping and unloading, and premarked garments avoided in-store price tagging. This cut the firm's order response time from three months to five days by 1996, and that's now down to 48 hours!

Thanks to *TWs*, retailers also can personalize service to your precise needs. Remember, your *TW* knows your tastes and preferences, body size, house layout and decor — all about you and your life. Again, Alfred Lynch, the now-retired CEO of **JCPenney International**, envisioned this info on a *Personal Preference Card*. By 2010, *TWs* might well have shrunk to card size. Today, you plug your *TW* into an in-store kiosk, and an interior design consultant, for example, can call up a virtual reality image of your living room. You see exactly how different colors and styles of curtains, decor, or furniture will look.

Or you can wear virtual reality eyeglasses to remodel your kitchen, selecting cupboards, countertops, and appliances from an electronic catalog to "see" how they fit. You can then "walk through" your dream kitchen, "turning on" voice-activated lights, appliances, and water taps, opening cupboard and fridge doors, and moving plates or groceries from one shelf to another.

Electrified Supermarket Shopping

Virtual reality also came to supermarket shopping. Ten years ago, **MarketWare** launched *Visionary Shopper*, the first system that let you browse store shelves, ask for info and advice, order, and pay — all from home.

Since 1997, millions of grocery shoppers "stroll" the aisles on a PC screen. Examining packages at eye-level, you zoom in on any shelf, grab any product, rotate the package, examine labels, compare prices and options, replace the package on the shelf, or drop it into an imaginary grocery cart. You pay with your *TW* and delivery comes in minutes by *FedEx Shuttle*. It's great for busy telecommuters, seniors, and shut-ins.

You can still shop in person at a supermarket. And have they changed! The grim, unfriendly, cavernous, discount warehouses either faded away when the "Super-Boom" made everybody rich, or they converted to video grocery warehouses. The **EZ-Shop** chain introduced touchscreen kiosks on which you chose the items you wanted before settling down to a free coffee and donut. Your purchases were picked out for you by robots from shelves in the warehouse — inside seven minutes — and taken to your car.

They now have a three-lane drive-through. You place your grocery order from your *TW* first, or at a drive-by kiosk. They hand you a free coffee and donut as you drive ahead into a complementary car wash. When your car emerges, they drop your bagged groceries into the trunk, and you drive off.

Other supermarkets, founded on the basis of do-it-yourself shopping in the 1980s, also became large and impersonal, offering no information and providing no help. Having lost touch with changing customer expectations, they too changed greatly in the mid-1990s. The top food retailers responded to consumer preferences for variety, premium quality, and freshness. They gave wide authority to store managers who — in tune with local neighborhood tastes — ordered fresh produce from nearby growers and food preparers.

Texas-based **Fiesta** set a trend of putting hydroponic gardens right in the produce section. This guaranteed quality and freshness — both still high-value issues for today's consumer. These firms also became specialty retailers, setting up delis, fresh meat, bulk food, and prepared foods sections. Orange County's **RanchMart** proved that people would pay more for fresh-picked locally grown organic food and fresh-cut meat.

Massive supermarkets are no longer intimidating. **Vons**, the California-based chain, has always operated vast superstores called *Pavilions*. But it has never lost the personal touch which made it famous. Every store is divided into boutique-like specialty "pavilions," each with its own staff and identity, such as a deli, bakery, dairy, coffee corner, and *tortilleria*.

The bakery, dairy, and *tortilleria* freshly make their own goods as you watch. The kids love to see the cows being milked in the glassed-in dairy. The milk is pasteurized and bottled on the spot, and they give out free samples. Talk about freshness! The floral section caters to everything from single flowers to full-scale weddings and gives gardening lessons.

Vons always tailored its stores to the taste and makeup of local markets, presenting a custom-array of products for each neighborhood. During the last decade's "Mini-Depression" the chain went one better than its discount warehouse competitors by opening *Expo* discount stores. Its *Super-Combo* format, first started in 1994, featured a full-service bank, a party store with catering facilities, a dry cleaner, a one-hour photo lab, and a pharmacy. It also opened separate *Tiangus* and *Shichang* (both mean "bazaar") chains to serve Hispanic/Latino and Chinese clientele in 1993 and 1996 respectively. It's now planning a *Souk* chain for Arab-Americans and other Muslims.

By the way, nobody clips coupons anymore. Since newspapers went electronic in 1999, supermarkets can no longer run wasteful ads or send junk mail with coupons for everyone. They use E-mail to send "electronic coupons" to the *TWs* of loyal customers whose buying habits show they will actually use them. When you present your *TW* at the checkout you get automatic credit for any discounts or in-store specials.

Super Valu even found a clever way to slash checkout time. In 1993 it gave customers a handheld gadget which let them scan their own items as they picked them off the shelf. The gizmo calculated the total bill and printed a receipt which customers paid at an express checkout.

With the arrival of computerized shopping carts, even that changed. The latest of these electronic wonders virtually ends the hassle of grocery shopping. **VideOcart**'s old version had an onboard screen which flashed store maps, recipes, sale items, ads for products, and instantly redeemable electronic coupons.

You saw product info on the screen as you passed by the product on the shelf, showing you the unit price, "green" rating, and nutritional value. And, by entering a hard-to-find product's name, the screen flashed its aisle and shelf location.

The newest carts, introduced in 2002, are even better. Their onboard scanners automatically give a comparative read on unit prices, "green" rating, nutrition level, and recipes. The scanner also triggers the payment system for finally selected items. At the same time, the store's computer collects info on your buying preferences to update the supermarket's data base.

Oh, to solve the privacy issue, they pay *you* a royalty for your info. President Al Gore forced *every* firm to do this when he started giving wristwatch *TWs* to schoolkids in 2001.

Best of all, there's no more checkout scanning or waiting! Payment is automatically made when you plug your *TW* into a slot on the cart. Electronic coupons and your weekly royalty fee are deducted, and any desired recipes are either beamed into your *TW* recipe file or printed out and handed to you as you whisk out the door.

Like I said, life's a breeze!

o o o

What brought all this about?

Caught in a whirlwind of change, most firms reeled from "future shock" throughout the 1970s and 1980s. They scorned planning, became trapped in short-term, narrow thinking, and ignored the changing customer.

Then the "Mini-Depression" of 1989-92 came along. That marked the "big shift" to the Info Economy — and changed all the rules.

Converging tele-computers shrank the world into a *Global Village* and simply reshaped society. *TWs* changed the way things work and how we shop and brought a global array of products into our living rooms electronically.

Record levels of non-European immigration and interracial marriage created a multicultural society.

The global ecology movement, spurred by the elections of Bill Clinton (1992) and Al Gore (2000), focused everyone on sustainable economics. Today, the entire world is enjoying a "Super-Boom" of record proportions.

These dramatic shifts forced companies to rethink their own futures. Those that recognized the brand-new future began to refocus. Visionary thinking not only became fashionable but futuristic companies saw that a "glocal" view of the market was essential.

Visionary companies learned how to predict and exploit the anomalies of the unfolding *Global Village* paradigm. They:

- Learned to trust people and gave them the power of information to serve customers better.

- Invested heavily in information technology.
- Learned that cooperative alliances were the best way to compete; even that capitalism could be socialistic.
- Found that ecological soundness was good for the planet *and* market share.
- Scrapped organizational hierarchy, regrouped into customer-focused teams, and wove info-intensive networks to mirror the market.
- Used "mass customization" to precisely tailor products and services to the cultural and personal preferences of individual buyers.
- Totally revamped their marketing mix and abandoned mass advertising.

Today's success stories literally "remade" themselves in the image of the future consumer.

To discover the specifics of how companies did (or didn't) change, let me "beam" you back to the mid-1990s.

A FIVE-STEP
"GLOCAL" MARKETING MODEL
for a "Global Village" Marketplace

The "glocal" market imperative cannot be evaded.
Even resolutely local firms must now compete with
global products in their own backyard. The global
marketplace is not elsewhere but everywhere.

—Henry Wendt, Chairman, **SmithKline Beecham**

Facing a brand-new future, tomorrow's market leaders are switching to *"glocal" marketing.*

"Glocal" is a word first suggested by Akio Morita, founder and chairman of **Sony** and Japan's corporate strategy guru. Instead of rushing to "globalize," he urged Japanese firms to adopt *"global localization"* — to market locally in a *Global Village* economy — because, he said:

The stiffest global market competition is local. To win in each market ... prod-
uct R&D and manufacturing must be customer-driven, as must marketing.

The very term *Global Village* is an incongruous global + local paradox; it is "glo-cal." Peter Drucker, in *Innovation and Entrepreneurship*, advised us to exploit the incongruity between reality *"as it is"* and *"as it's assumed to be."* Surefire market success will go to companies which exploit the *Global Village* anomaly. A 1992 ad campaign by **IBM** posed the challenge:

Somehow the word "foreign" seems foreign these days. The world is smaller,
so people are thinking bigger, beyond borders. Yet cultures will always be dif-
ferent. And that's the paradox of global business — the need to be global and
local at the same time.

Glocal marketing solves the quandary. It synergizes global and local marketing strategies to exceed glocal customer expectations. A glocal brand — being both particular *and* universal — has most market value. Thus, though no two customers are alike, a glocal brand will satisfy individual buyers worldwide.

Even **Coca-Cola**, which owns the world's [#]1 brand name, switched to glocal marketing in 1992. Now pursuing a *Multi-Local* strategy, it banned the use of the words *domestic* and *foreign* companywide. Secretly, **Coke** has long varied soft drink sweeteners to suit local tastes. Of course, it also changes its packaging to appeal to different language markets. But it's also begun to localize its advertising, even in North America. David Sanderson, **Coke**'s Canadian marketing VP, asserts:

Few firms can do global advertising effectively. There are few brands where global standardization makes sense.

Leaders Switch to "Glocal" Marketing

This book is for executives who, like those at **Coke**, seek to reposition their companies in the new marketplace. It offers a **Five-Step "Glocal" Marketing Model** of futuristic strategies for you to follow.

Companies already switching to this model are exemplified throughout the book, their names highlighted in **bold** type. Based on our research at Glocal Marketing Incorporated, 30 companies (*tabled*) are leading the switch to glocal marketing.

Drawing on the glocal strategies of these and other firms, by design this book is crammed with brief, eyeopening case examples (330 of them!) and succinct executive sound-bite quotes (60 of them!).

Many names will be familiar. But this is the first time you'll see them in "glocal" perspective, their strategies garnered from interviews with executives at the companies concerned.

Top 30 "Glocal" Marketing Leaders

• AT&T	• Ben & Jerry's	• Benetton
• Boeing	• Coca-Cola	• Federal Express
• Ford Motor	• Four Seasons Hotels	• Kodak
• Kraft General Foods	• Marriott Hotels	• Matsushita
• McDonald's	• Motorola	• Nike
• Nissan	• Northern Telecom	• J.C.Penney
• Pepsi-Cola	• Procter & Gamble	• Rosenbluth Travel
• Sanwa Bank	• Saturn (part of GM)	• Sony
• The Body Shop	• Time-Warner	• Toyota
• Vons	• Wal-Mart	• Xerox

All these examples and quotes are needed, for two reasons: to convince you of the glocal marketing trend; and to persuade you to join the movement. These firms show that glocal marketing is neither academic theory nor business fad. It's a new and vital direction in the new *Global Village* marketplace.

Customers always vote with their money. Future consumers will swarm to glocal companies which understand their new preferences. This book aims to help you attract them, keep them buzzing happily in *your* hive, and harvest the honey.

Before overviewing the model, let's further understand why so many companies are suddenly turning to glocal marketing.

Beyond the "Globalization" Delusion

In the early 1980s, some marketing experts forecast that, as countries industrialized, basic consumer needs and behaviors would become similar. They said that — excepting minor changes to adjust for peculiar situations — the same product could be sold with the same appeal in all markets. Indeed, Harvard University's Theodore Levitt blatantly asserted:

The modern global corporation...instead of adapting to superficial and even entrenched differences within and between nations...will seek sensibly to force suitably standardized products and practices on the entire globe.

This bombastic call for standardized global marketing was presumptuous. Belatedly seeing that rapid global communication was creating the *Global Village* that Marshall McLuhan forecast 20 years before, Levitt leapt to the wrong conclusion. He said this would homogenize customer behavior worldwide and that market success demanded standardization. By converting economies of scale (in production, distribution, marketing, and management) into lower world prices, he said firms would *"decimate competitors."* Hence, strategies developed in Manhattan could be applied virtually intact anywhere on the planet.

This total misread of market forces quickly caught the imagination of many advertising agencies and their major clients. Indeed, Saatchi & Saatchi positioned itself as the agency to help clients *"seize the opportunity for world brands."* These firms wrongly assumed that standardized global products should automatically be promoted, advertised, and sold in a standard way.

It turns out that, as the world shrinks, we *Global Villagers* are rebelling *against* homogenization. Recognizing his gaffe, Levitt later admitted that his claims of rampant homogenization were extreme. *"Of course I'm exaggerating,"* he said, *"but when implementing my ideas, I assume my readers use common sense and prudence."* He claimed that when you're trying to change human behavior, you *"don't present people with judiciously balanced arguments."*

Coming from a Harvard professor of marketing who regularly espouses his views in *Harvard Business Review*, that's an astonishing admission!

Fortunately for marketing, Northwestern University's Philip Kotler rejected Levitt's homogenized marketing approach as stillborn. Kotler reasoned — correctly — that the world was becoming *less* homogenized and that *"globalization doesn't mean the end of market segments"* and that only a small proportion of the world's products could be branded globally.

Let's be honest, the adoption of another society's products does *not* mean its cultural and social patterns are also adopted. One billion Chinese may drink **Coca-Cola** every day of their lives. That will assure **Coke's** [#]1 brand status, but its Chinese consumers will never align their cultural and social lifestyle with that of America.

On the contrary, as noted already and detailed later, **Coca-Cola** itself fully recognizes that standardization and homogenization don't work. We've entered a new and exciting business future — a future where glocal marketing will soon be mainstream. The challenge of maintaining local market initiative with global products will increase the need for glocal marketing. Locally tailored products will proliferate.

Glocal marketing thus is a strategic leap beyond globalization. It's time to abandon that dangerous, one-dimensional delusion. So, do yourself a big favor: forget everything you've heard about globalization and switch to glocal marketing and yet another anomaly, "mass customization."

"Mass Customization"

In the anomalous *Global Village*, key strategic leverage has shifted. As Marshall McLuhan forecast, it is now *"just about as cheap to turn out a million differing objects as a million exact duplicates."* More important, customers know that!

Hence, companies must use "mass customization," tailoring products and services to exceed individual customer expectations. Contrary to Levitt's assertion, it is companies that match *local* market nuances with *global* product and service standards that will "decimate competitors."

Most firms are oblivious to this new customer-driven marketing dynamic. Instead of focusing on individual consumer needs, they are still playing catch-up with the Japanese in production-line quality. Meanwhile, Japan has perfected quality manufacturing and shifted to glocal marketing.

Eventually, of course, any truly competitive firm will offer flawless quality. Once perfection is commonplace, then what? Quality alone won't boost market share. Quality will only improve when you focus on new customer needs. Yet *Total Quality Management (TQM)* focuses on the manufacturing process, not market results. Quality must be seen through the eyes of the customer, not the production manager. Quality is a marketing goal, not a manufacturing one. It should run through the company's blood.

Candidly, to achieve market-driven quality, separate quality departments should be abolished. After all, **Xerox** won both the *Baldrige Award* and Japan's *Deming Prize* without a quality department. How can you argue with *that*? Richard Palermo, **Xerox**'s vice president in charge of quality, asserts:

Quality programs fail because firms set up isolated quality departments. We use cross-functional teams to attack quality problems, most of which result from functional foxholes. Each employee is responsible for quality. We empower them to exceed customer expectations. Quality is simply our way of doing business — one that is totally focused on the customer.

"Info-Glocalization" Transforms Customer Relations

The main reason it is important to focus on the needs of *individual* consumers is that the era of *mass* production and *mass* consumption is over. The Information Revolution is reconfiguring every dimension of our world, including local producer-consumer relationships.

These relationships, and the structure of markets, always change parallel to changes in technology and in society at large.

Consider the following shifts in marketing from the Agricultural through the Industrial to today's Information Age.

• Agricultural Age = Local Village Market

In the Agricultural Age, the producer *was* the consumer. About 90% of the people lived and worked in the countryside. With the family farm the basic economic unit of society, people grew their own food and provided for themselves.

Society revolved around the *local* community and its village market. Few such places still exist today. There was but one general store, a few vendors at the market, and a dozen shops on main street in the nearest town. The average shop had less than 500 square feet of space and carried fewer than 300 products. All the shopkeepers were well-known and trusted. Shopping was a pleasant, relaxing experience.

Marketing was *local* and based on *individual* consumer tastes and buying patterns.

• Industrial Age = City/Suburban Shopping Malls

In the Industrial Age, a few *mass* producers met most people's needs. Specialized trades emerged and economic activity was synchronized to machine time, the clock. Henry Ford introduced mass production, standardization, and centralization.

People flocked to the city to work, and the automobile revolution slowly shaped and reshaped urban society. Main street shops were finally replaced by malls in sprawling suburbs. Today, in a city of one million people, there are 15 million square feet of retail space, eight thousand stores, and one million products to choose from. One **Wal-Mart** *HyperMart* covers 130,000 square feet and offers 110,000 different products. Shopping is nerve-wracking, and none of the salespeople know you.

Marketing is *urban/regional/national* and mechanically driven by the *mass* production and *mass* consumption of *standard* products.

• Information Age = Electronic *Global Village* Market

In the rapidly unfolding Information Age, most people will live, learn, work, play, shop, and do business anyplace, anytime — all electronically. Flexible producers will serve a *Global Village* full of *individual* consumers who increasingly demand *customized* products and services.

Product and service design is moving toward *mass customization*, with *global* standards being flexible enough to accommodate individualized, *local* customer needs. Society and its markets will reform around cellular info-network designs. Business will be driven by the swift movement and synthesis of information. It is the age of "informed," real-time shopping.

The new market is both *centralized* and *decentralized*, with info-glocalized producers and consumers. All marketing must *"glocalize."*

Technical and socioeconomic change thus are locked in a cycle of evolution. Automakers put buggy-whip makers out of business and made drive-ins and drive-throughs possible. In turn, drive-in movies were replaced by drive-home video tapes.

With the merging of TVs, phones, and computers into *TeleCom Wallets*, everything will change again. Business empires are already being built on the replacement of an automobile-based "drive-in, drive-through" merchandising system, with a "stay-home, see-through" system made possible by the advent of virtual reality.

Virtual Reality, another glocal anomaly, is inherently theatrical. It lets you take part in dramatic and emotional events — like shopping. It will let shoppers use their senses to build the product of their personal dreams, spontaneously in their minds. It puts consumers in control, empowering them to shape the entire production-consumption process to their precise needs.

Customer-Driven "Glocal" Marketing Strategies
Suddenly, the *Global Village* paradigm becomes, if you will, marketing's virtual reality. This changes all the rules.

Until the 1970s, marketing was purely product-driven. Most companies used slick sales pitches to ram mass-made products down consumers' throats. It was a supply-push market; the company was king. In the 1980s, encouraged by Levitt's globalization edict, this deadend marketing approach was extended multinationally. Mass product and service providers tried to call the shots, peddling style over quality. In their best-selling *In Search of Excellence*, Peters and Waterman asserted:

Despite all the lip service...the customer is either ignored or considered a bloody nuisance.

In frantic response to their failed global efforts, companies tried to segment the market and get "close to the customer." But products remained standardized, and buyers stayed poorly understood — and mostly ignored. Consumers demanded Japanese-like durability, and the market finally became quality-driven. However, overly focused on "quality," firms failed to exercise Japanese-style "glocal" control over their marketing mix.

As **Sony** and others have shown, glocal firms use a strategy of *global* scope through *local* scale. As they *locally* market their brands via *global* info-networks operating at light speed, they forge unbeatable customer links. They "go glocal" with a Glocal Marketing Model.

The Five-Step "Glocal" Marketing Model

To give you a quick grasp of the Five-Step "Glocal" Marketing Model, it is overviewed here. Each step has four subelements, creating a 5 x 4 matrix *(see table, overleaf)*.

Step One: Forecast Marketplace Trends
The model first forecasts major market trends:
- **Socio-Cultural Divergence:** An emerging "Salad Bowl" (i.e., multi-cultural) and aging marketplace.
- **Tele-Computer Convergence:** Computer/information revolution, merging telephones, TVs, and computers.
- **Coming 25-Year "Super-Boom":** Info Age takeoff brings economic upsurge and record prosperity.
- **Issues-Driven Politics:** Widespread concern with various public issues overrides political ideology.

Step Two: Predict Consumer Behavior
The next step is to deduce the impact of societal trends on customer behavior and expectations:
- **Culture-Based Behavior:** Multicultural society reinforces culture-driven buyer behavior.
- **Techno-Sophistication:** Info revolution leads buyers to expect highly sophisticated product and service delivery.
- **Value-Based Buying:** Boom times plus "hangover" from recent "Mini-Depression" lead to value-based buying.
- **Virtuous Lifestyles:** Pursuit of ecologically sound and socially responsible lifestyles.

FIVE-STEP "GLOCAL" MARKETING MODEL					
	Step 1	**Step 2**	**Step 3**	**Step 4**	**Step 5**
	Forecast Marketplace Trends (p.37)	Predict Consumer Behavior (p.55)	Master Core Competencies (p.68)	Create an Info-Network Culture (p.93)	Revamp the Market Mix (New 4-Ps) (p.118)
Social "High-Touch" Dynamic	Socio-Cultural Divergence (p.37)	Culture-Based Behavior (p.55)	Employee Empower-ment (p.68)	Passionate Caring (p.93)	"Mass-Custom-ized" Product (p.118)
Technical "High-Tech" Dynamic	Tele-computer Conver-gence (p.41)	Techno-Sophis-tication (p.62)	Proprietary Products (p.74)	Powerful Commun-ication (p.103)	AnyTime + AnyPlace (p.124)
Economic "High-Value" Dynamic	Coming 25-Year "Super Boom" (p.47)	Value-Based Buying (p.63)	Info-Intensity (p.78)	Cooper-ating to Compete (p.107)	Total Value Price (p.135)
Political "High-Virtue" Dynamic	Issues-Driven Politics (p.51)	Virtuous Lifestyles (p.65)	Commun-ity Ethics (p.84)	Societal Commit-ment (p.110)	Precise Position-ing (p.139)

(Page numbers are provided for your ready reference)

Step Three: Master Core Competencies

Marketplace and consumer behavioral changes must be matched with a series of core marketing competencies:

- **Employee Empowerment:** Educate people and authorize them to act entrepreneurially in serving customers.
- **Proprietary Products:** Use unique R&D capabilities to offer innovative products with unexpected features.
- **Information Intensity:** Become an info-driven, real-time company offering value-added products.
- **Community Ethics:** Be socially responsible to the glocal community on all customer-relevant issues.

Step Four: Create an Info-Network Culture

Having mastered such core competencies, glocal companies will regroup into a cellular info-network that is built on a corporate culture which is rooted in four inspiring principles:

- **Passionate Caring:** Self-directed teams care passionately about customers and treat them as honored guests.
- **Powerful Communication:** Information flows unimpeded to coordinate action closest to the customer.
- **Cooperating to Compete:** Supplier networks and strategic alliances are forged, creating added value for the customer.
- **Societal Commitment:** Offering glocal community leadership, companies operate in a customer-relevant way.

Step Five: Revamp the Market Mix (New 4-Ps)

Lastly, a glocal company will develop a glocal marketing mix which reflects the changed marketplace. The new 4-Ps are:

- **"Mass-Customized" Product:** Beyond the global homogenization myth, tailoring products for individual buyers.
- **AnyTime+AnyPlace:** Beyond the linear channels myth, serving buyers wherever they might be, timelessly.
- **Total Value Price:** Beyond the discount pricing myth, tailoring costs/prices to local market situations.
- **Precise (1:1) Positioning:** Beyond the global advertising and promotion myths, presenting single consumers with personally relevant (1:1) glocal product information.

Checklists for "Glocal" Marketers

The Five-Step Model is detailed in the book's five sections. Each section concludes with a "Checklist" of outcomes, strategic implications, lessons, and tips to help you emulate the glocal market leaders. After reading this book, you should be well on your way to becoming a glocal marketer. You will learn:

- ✓ Which major forces — global and local — will reshape the marketplace in the late 1990s and beyond.
- ✓ Which market demands will change, and what will be the new expectations of your customers.
- ✓ Which core competencies your company will need to succeed, and how to develop them.
- ✓ How to reform your corporate structure around a team-based, cellular info-network, and how to develop a glocal marketing culture.
- ✓ Why you need a brand-new glocal marketing mix for your company — and how to develop it.

In sum, you'll be ready to lead your company to success in the 21st-century's glocal marketing era. Let's begin with Step One.

FORECAST MARKETPLACE TRENDS

The mythological homogeneous America is gone.
We are a mosaic of minorities.

—Joel Weiner, SVP Marketing, **Kraft General Foods**

The glocal era will be radically different. Massive global forces of change — social, technical, economic, political — are reconfiguring the world into a *Global Village*. The Information Revolution in particular is putting the global economy through a wrenching process of "creative destruction" — redeciding who is going to make (and consume) what, where, when, and why.

In North America, we can discern this brand-new future in the four broad trends reviewed in this section:

1. Socio-Cultural Divergence
2. Tele-Computer Convergence
3. Coming 25-Year "Super-Boom"
4. Issues-Driven Politics

1. Socio-Cultural Divergence

A key dynamic of our new marketplace is social change itself. We tend to forget that societies — and markets — literally regenerate themselves. Yet we think of ourselves as a homogeneous "melting pot" which hardly changes. This attitude has been reinforced by an overfascination with the "Baby Boom" generation which, despite its impressive size, is still only a third of the total market. Marketers in particular, perhaps because many of them are male "Baby Boomers," still treat America as a "white-European male" mass market.

Not only is the "melting pot" a myth, but the mass market is splintering into segments as small as one person. Individual consumption habits are shattering assumptions about segmentable behavior. After all, buying habits are as individual as fingerprints. Consumer behavior is driven by each person's unique biographical subculture which, in turn, is largely determined by three general yet personally diverse elements:

• Ethnic Identity
• Generational Identity
• Gender Identity

Ethnic Identity

We are not (and never have been) a "melting pot" society. You can't melt people down. Root culture lasts for generations, if not forever. We've also tended to give the "melting pot" a European identity. To continue to give the market a European heritage will be a fatal error. We are fast becoming a microcosm of the *Global Village*, with the nonwhite groups growing much faster than the Caucasian.

Apart from the patently obvious and fast-growing vibrant African-American and Hispanic/Latino segments, nonwhite birthrates are much higher than average so that 40% of teens (that is, tomorrow's consumers) are nonwhite. As they age, the market will become even more multicultural.

There also is a dramatic shift in immigration. During the 1960s, new immigrants made up only 10% of North America's population growth, versus 33% in the 1970s. This rose to 40% in the 1980s. To replenish our aging society, we will continue to absorb record numbers of immigrants, most of whom will be non-Caucasian. Since 1970, 40% of immigrants were Hispanic/Latino, 35% were Asian, and only 12% were European.

This trend will continue. The Hispanic/Latino sector of the U.S. population grew 53% in the 1980s and will grow a further 35% during the 1990s. The number of Asians doubled in the 1980s and will almost do so again in this decade.

Forecasting "Glocal" America

	1980	1990	2000
	Millions	Millions (% Inc.)	Millions (% Inc.)
Hispanic/Latino	15	22 (53)	30 (35)
African-American	27	30 (13)	34 (14)
Asian-American	3	7 (100)	12 (71)

(Source: Urban Institute)

As a result of these trends, whites will become the minority in many areas. California will be 50% Hispanic/Latino and Asian by the year 2000. By then, 42% of California children will be Caucasian, 36% will be Hispanic/Latino, 13% Asian, and 9% will be African-American. Within a generation, New York City will be 35% Hispanic/Latino, and within two generations, it will be 41% Hispanic/Latino and 15% Asian. As well, immigrants usually are young adults and thus create new families. As a result, many future households will be nonwhite.

There also are 1,100 mosques across the U.S., up from only 104 in 1960, with some 5 million practicing Muslims. Of these, 48% are African-American (including 6% African immigrants), 31% are from south-central Asia (India, Pakistan, Bangladesh, Sri Lanka, Iran, Afghanistan, or Turkey), while another

12% are Arabs. About a million Muslims live in California and another million in New York-New Jersey. Soon after the year 2000, Muslims could outnumber America's 6 million Jews, making Islam the nation's second-largest faith.

Marketers also mistakenly think of Canada (other than Quebec) as bilingual English-French. In truth, only 14% of Canadians claim to be bilingual, including Quebecers. In Toronto, 59% of residents have ethnic origins other than British or French — up from 45% in 1986. While there are other important European groups, the Chinese (mostly Cantonese), Hindustani (India and Pakistan), and other Asian immigrants are the fastest-growing sectors. By the year 2004, non-white segments will more than double, and close to half of Toronto's population and two-fifths of Vancouver's will be nonwhite.

As well, of course, 85 million Mexicans have joined the North American Free Trade Agreement (NAFTA) to create what I call the "AMEXICANA" (America+Mexico+Canada) marketplace. Within two decades, Mexico's population will be 105 million. By then, as in western Europe today, there will be a free flow of goods, services, capital, technology, workers, and consumers in all directions across the continent.

As this occurs, the self-feeding spiral of intercultural mixing will continue. Even racial lines are blurring as mixed-race marriages and births increase noticeably. Between 1970 and 1991, the number of interracial married couples tripled to 1.1 million and multiethnic babies now account for 4% of births. As these numbers increase again in the 1990s, the social meaning of "race" will undergo subtle shifts and the family will become globally extended.

In the past, when cultures made contact, the stronger usually controlled or swallowed up the weaker. Strong cultures still impose on weaker ones, but today, each culture is both the source and adopter of different values, ideas, and innovations. Culture is a product of social mixing — and we are mixing like never before. The *global* flow of people and information into *local* markets are forming a multi-ethnic *glocal* smorgasbord.

Generational Identity

Having largely ignored ethnographics, most marketers remain infatuated by demographics and psychographics, the age and mindset of simplistic groups. In fact, the two factors are interrelated, and not just because of people changing their minds about things as they age.

While no generation can be given precise boundaries, in North America there are discernable 16-17-year birth cycles of about one generation in length. Most people survive into their fifth generation but they can best be defined in terms of their activity during childhood, young adulthood, and midlife — that time of life when they grew up, raised their own children, and became socially mature.

Each generation thus bears a strong imprint of the milieu in which it is born and raised. This is particularly important to consider in an immigrant society like North America. Again, the "melting pot" mentality has created a false assumption that everyone was born and raised here.

The Five "Marketplace 2004" Generations

While no generation has precise boundaries, most scholars suggest similar divisions. Demographers agree the "Baby Boom" generation spanned the high-fertility years of 1946-64, and sociologists define generations largely in terms of social milieu. Looking toward the year 2004, we at Glocal Marketing Incorporated define generational types as follows:

- **"By-the-Book" (born 1911-28)**

    These WWI/Prohibition-era great-grandparents account for 14% of the market, but this share will fall to 7% by 2004.

- **"By-the-Clock" (born 1929-45)**

    These Depression/WWII-era grandparents will still form 15% of the market in 2004.

- **"Baby Boom" (born 1946-64)**

    One-third of the market today, the postwar TV-era Baby Boom joins the 45-year-plus category daily and, by 2004, most of them will be grandparents.

- **"Generation X" (born 1965-82)**

    This 50-million strong market, though growing through immigration, is still shadowed (ignored?) by "Baby Boomers."

- **"Real-Time" (born 1983-2000)**

    The tele-computer kids will lead 21st-century society, and, through immigration, their number will grow beyond 2000.

Remembering that consumers are individually influenced by many factors, we will consider the purchasing behavior of each "generation" when we get to Step Two of our marketing model.

Gender Identity

Obviously, another key element of consumer identity is gender. And it goes without saying that 52% of society is female. It also is evident that male and female consumer behavior is different. Yet many still think of the marketplace as a male domain for anything but products made purely for women.

The so-called women's movement, which is a natural part of postindustrialization, has created a trans-gender society. The coming of the Info Age has so changed family economics that there is less need for childbearing and more chance for women to gain higher education and enter the mainstream.

In 1970, for example, women earned only 23% of bachelor degrees in North America. By 1980, this doubled to 46% and reached 56% in 1993, enabling women to develop careers, to have financial independence, and to move into positions of power. The MBA graduates of the last decade were 48% male and 52% female. They will be the ones running tomorrow's companies.

Again, in 1970, less than 1% of business travelers were women, but they now account for 46% of airline frequent-flyers. The number of women holders of **American Express** cards increased from a mere 70,000 in 1972 to more than 8 million in 1993. The same year, women leased or bought exactly half of all new cars in America.

In short, marketplace power and influence has become a trans-gender affair.

2. Tele-Computer Convergence

Clearly, another major market force is the info-tech revolution. Information and communications technology are transforming all aspects of our lives, creating a world where distance and place become far less important. The next decade will see computer, phone, and TV networks converge into an info-network of three components:
- Information Superhighway
- Electronic Cottage
- "TeleCom Wallet"

Information Superhighway
The so-called "information superhighway" will dramatically alter the way business is done and how markets operate. All forms of communication (spoken, written, printed, or imaged) can be digitized and sent over the same fiber optic phone line.

The superhighway's emergence is marked by the frenzy of takeover and merger activity in the telephone, computer, television, and telecommunications sectors.

Particularly significant was **Bell Atlantic**'s attempted take-over of **TCI**, the world's largest cable firm. **Bell Atlantic** also won a U.S. court battle to make video programs rather than merely carry programs for other firms. It aims to have 9 million of its 11 million customers equipped for video on demand by 1999. Unless Congress restores a ban to stop telephone companies (telcos) from buying local cable firms, the telcos may now do so.

Indeed, in early 1994, the Clinton administration urged a House Judiciary panel to pass a bill to let local telcos offer long-distance service and sell related equipment. The bill also would allow phone and cable companies to invade each other's turf. This would move us toward Vice President Al Gore's vision of the information superhighway *(see box on page 43)*.

Deregulation of these industries will let each enter the other's business. For example:

- **Local telcos** (such as **Bell Atlantic** and **Ameritech**) will provide long-distance and interactive video services.
- **Long-distance telcos** (such as **AT&T**, **Sprint**, and **MCI**) will provide local calling and interactive video.
- **Cable TV operators** (such as **TCI** and **Viacom**) will provide phone service over their lines.
- **Computer/microchip/software makers** (such as **IBM**, **Apple**, **AT&T**, **Motorola**, **Intel**, and **Microsoft**) will supply the newly integrated interactive telecom systems.
- **Media, TV-shopping, and entertainment companies** (such as **NBC**, **QVC**, **Paramount**, and **Time-Warner**) will provide much of the info content.

For example, **Time Warner**'s *Interactive Group* service (being tested in Orlando and described in the *"Shopping in 2004"* scenario at the front of the book) splits the cable signal for TVs or PCs. Homes also get a color printer so they can receive product ads, coupons, and brochures on request.

On the opposite coast, **Time Warner** is spending $5 billion with **U.S.West** to upgrade its cable network with fiberoptic wire and interactive technology by 1998. And **Pacific Bell** plans to have a superhighway available to 50% of Californians by 2003 and to all California homes by 2015. The broadband network will carry voice, interactive video, and data services. Consumers will access an unlimited array of healthcare, education, entertainment, social service, business enhancement, government and consumer services, and information. By 1997, with an all-digital network already in place, **Pacific Bell** claims California's "info-structure" will be second to none.

In Canada, Ontario is pursuing a similar vision to *"be the best place in the world to live, work, learn, and do business."* With almost 40% of Canada's population, Ontario already has more fiberoptic cable per person than anywhere else in the world, with fiberoptic "rings" around and through all major cities. It is speeding the development of high-capacity, multi-media networks to connect homes, offices, schools, factories, and labs across the province.

In neighboring Quebec, **Vidéotron** already provides ITV news and sports, plus video games and info-services, to 220,000 homes in Montreal and the Atlantic provinces. Its subscriber base doubled between 1990 and 1993, reaching a 27% market penetration. In 1994, **Vidéotron** formed a huge consortium called **UBI** (pronounced *"you-bee"* and meaning "universality, bidirectionality, interactivity"). Another 34,000 homes in Quebec's Saguenay region will be served by mid-1995.

VICE PRESIDENT AL GORE'S VISION
OF THE INFORMATION SUPERHIGHWAY

Imagine you had a device that combined a telephone, a TV, a camcorder, and a personal computer. No matter where you went or what time it was, your child could see you and talk to you, you could watch a replay of your team's last game, you could browse through the latest additions to the library, or you could find the best prices in town on groceries, furniture, clothes — whatever you need.

Imagine further the dramatic changes in your life if:

- The best schools, teachers, and courses were available to all students, regardless of geography, distance, resources, or disability;
- Art, literature, and science were available everywhere, not just in large institutions or big-city libraries and museums;
- Services that improve the health-care system and respond to other important social needs were available on-line, without waiting in line, when and where you needed them;
- You could live anywhere without foregoing opportunities for useful and fulfilling employment, by telecommuting to your office via an electronic highway instead of by car, bus, or train;
- Small manufacturers could get orders from all over the world electronically — with detailed specifications — in a form that machines could use to produce the necessary items;
- You could see the latest movies, play the hottest video games, or bank and shop from home whenever you chose;
- You could obtain government information directly or through local libraries, apply for and receive government benefits electronically, and get in touch with government officials easily;
- Individual government agencies, business, and other entities could exchange information electronically, thereby reducing paperwork and improving service.

(Source: **Vice President Al Gore**, from *The National Information Infrastructure: The Administration's Agenda for Action*, Version 1.0; September 15, 1993.)

The final goal is to reach 80% of Québec's 1.6 million homes by 2002. Consumers will access the services via a cable-TV network but will only pay for whatever services or goods they buy. They get a free decoder unit, personalized "smart" card and reader, a special converter wand, and a small transaction printer.

UBI partners are U.S. media giant **Hearst Corp.**, **Canada Post**, **Hydro-Québec**, **Loto-Québec**, and **National Bank of Canada**. This brings a media firm, a post office, a electric utility, a government agency, and a bank onto the information superhighway. **UBI** thus offers two-way electronic services to let people browse, shop, bank, vote, buy lottery tickets — even adjust their energy consumption — from an easy chair.

Electronic Cottage

The home already is fast-becoming Alvin Toffler's *"Electronic Cottage."* By 1993, by all estimates, at least 28% of North American households had at least one member who worked at or from home — and 70% of them had computers.

Computers "empower" their users to collect and send knowledge, bypassing other channels. There are 64,000 computer bulletin board services (BBSs) in North America, up from zero in 1986. Open to anyone with a $100 modem to send and receive data over a phone line, 20 million people already use them. Large BBSs such as *Exec-PC* now rival *CompuServe*, the service owned by **H&R Block**, which alone has 300+ BBSs and a million subscribers in 92 countries.

Many BBSs link with the **Internet** global network which switches "electronic mail" (E-mail) messages between BBSs, avoiding phone call charges. More than 1.5 million computers on **Internet** link 10,000 networks in more than 50 countries. Each year, **Internet** doubles its traffic volume and user base, growing faster than any telecom system ever built, including the phone network. Users could easily top 100 million by 1998. When more firms realize they can send documents instantly from a PC cheaper than by fax, **Internet** use will skyrocket. Indeed, the fax will become as obsolete as the telex, and, instead of a fax number, you'll print an E-mail address on your business card.

The *Global Village* comes to the desktop. We're now linked to global society and inevitably influenced by it, and not just by *CNN* television. About 600 satellites encircle the planet. These "tom-tom drums" of the *Global Village* keep us "in the know" as the world erupts into each home.

In 1994, **Hughes'** *DirecTv* and **Hubbard's** *U.S. Satellite Broadcasting (USSB)* began beaming 150 crystal-clear channels, including 35 cable networks, 60 pay-per-view movie channels, and 30 sports channels. Using digital signals, the service provides sound and pictures with the fidelity and crispness of laser-disk movies. The firm expects to have 10 million subscribers by the year 2000.

With an 18-inch, pizza-size, window-sill antenna dish and a TV-top decoder, viewers use a remote control and "smart card" to track pay-per-view movies.

USSB also will introduce what it calls *"Mini-Mass"* pay-per-view channels to deliver special interest programs to small niche audiences, such as opera fans.

Tele-computers will also answer the quandary of how to fill a 500-channel TV network. Cable can transmit data at far higher speeds than phones, and integrated multimedia services can deliver TV-quality video and stereo sound through computer-TVs. The necessary hardware is already converging. For example, **Compaq**'s *Presario* series of compact PCs look more like TVs and combine a 14-inch color monitor, answering machine, and fax modem into a single tele-computer unit.

"TeleCom Wallet"

The *TeleCom Wallet* described in the opening *"Shopping in 2004"* scenario is no dream. The necessary technologies are converging, with computers, TVs, VCRs, cellphones, modems, fax machines, and photocopiers being integrated into a single "info-appliance." By 2000, the *PC Memory Card* consortium (250+ firms) will have created a gizmo that will make science fiction hero *Dick Tracy*'s wristwatch phone look childish.

Already, the new *Sage* (due out from **AT&T** in 1995) will coordinate information flowing to/from the phone, answering machine, fax, TV, VCR, PC, videogame player, and video camera. The *Sage* will use slot-in cards that either mimic one of these other appliances or connect to one.

This fusing of hardware and software will constantly speed up the pace of life. By the late 1990s, pocket-sized computers, expert software, interactive TV (ITV), and virtual reality (VR) will transform life yet again. Intelligent computers will speak and hear — and "think" and "decide." The voice box will replace the keyboard. Even today, voice-activated computers can be operated from across the planet by telephone. Soon, automatic translators will erase language barriers.

Hard to believe?

Any scientific breakthrough is akin to magic; people are always skeptical about it. Its socioeconomic impacts and market potentials are always underrated, even by experts. In 1943, for example, the late Thomas Watson Jr., then CEO of **IBM**, forecast a world market of five computers!

Today, a new desktop, laptop, or palmtop PC goes into use every two seconds. In 1985, there was one 64K-chip per person worldwide. Today, 64K-chips are obsolete. By 2004, there will be 12,800 megabytes per person — a 20,000-fold increase in 20 years! Even with today's computers, which make billions of decisions a second, "instant" loses all meaning and "location" is incidental. This is the world of "tele-presence."

The Info Age is access-driven. And the important devices are those that connect us. What's more, people having tasted "wireless" phones, the age of "wired" phones is over. People want total freedom from "tethered" phones; they want "AnyPlace" mobility and connectivity.

AT&T invented the cellphone in 1946. When the company was broken up in 1984, it insisted there would be fewer than 900,000 wireless phones in use by 2000. Today, the U.S. cellular industry adds 10,500 subscribers daily and, by 1993, there were 12 million cellphone subscribers spending $8 billion a year — expected to top $16 billion by 2000. Two-thirds of homes will have cellphones by 2000 — and **AT&T** will have sold 200 million units worldwide.

Recognizing cellular's future, **AT&T**'s 1993 takeover of **McCaw Cellular** created a U.S.-wide wireless network, blurring the line between local and long-distance calling and allowing **AT&T** to provide long-distance cellular service directly, bypassing local telcos. More than 60 million potential users live within **McCaw**'s network which covers a third of metro America. **MCI**, **Sprint**, and other telcos have forged similar cellular alliances.

These consortia also will bid on radio licenses for personal cellular services (such as pocket phones, pagers, and handheld computers) to be auctioned by the FCC. Consumers account for only 15% of the 16 million pagers in use, but personal use is growing 25% annually. To tap this market, **Motorola**'s new credit-card-size version can be inserted in the **Apple** *Newton* or **Tandy** *Zoomer*. The firm also sells a cellphone pager and a voice-pager that takes messages like an answering machine.

Info-networks thus make "location" irrelevant. We live in an AnyPlace world of banking without banks, shops without stores, inventory without warehouses, conferences without meeting rooms, schools without classrooms, libraries without books, and management without headquarters. Everything occurs *within* the info-network.

The *Desktop News* **IBM-NBC-NuMedia** venture, for example, serves business users with PCs on their desks, sending *NBC* and *CNBC* video news stories by satellite. Stories are electronically tagged according to topic and a central computer sends pretailored reports to your PC.

Hearst/ABC-Viacom's *Pyramed Network* is an interactive computer-based network for doctors' homes. It competes with **Whittle**'s fledgling *Medical Network News*, a satellite-fed interactive news show beamed to doctors' offices.

Cablevision Systems and **Digital Equipment Corp (DEC)** offer *Ethernet* computer networking to New York businesses, hospitals, libraries, and employees working from home. Users can share data between their computers as much as 70 miles apart. **DEC** is also running similar trials with **TCI** in California and with **Columbia Cable** in Oregon.

In this world of "electronic commerce," people can buy when and where they feel like it. In future, *all* markets — not just global financial ones — will be "open" for business 24 hours a day, year round. As with banking machine networks, the electronic system itself is both the place and time of business, whatever the type of business. The info-network *is* the marketplace where customers now "gather" to buy.

Indeed, even money is going electronic. Technology always changes the medium of exchange used in society, as follows:

Evolution of "Money"

Artifacts	Barter ⟶ Shells ⟶ Tokens
Metal	Coins
Paper	Paper Money ⟶ IOUs ⟶ Checks
Plastic	Credit Cards ⟶ Debit Cards
ATM	Cash ⟶ Electronic Bill Payment
Phone/PC/TV	Tele-Money
TeleCom Wallet	Digital Money

Today's banks don't so much have account holders as card holders. In a way, a plastic bank card *is* a bank account. In future, your *TeleCom Wallet* will *be* your bank account.

3. Coming 25-Year "Super-Boom"

The third major force changing the market is today's disruptive "big shift" to tomorrow's prosperous Information Economy. The stock crash of 1987 gave most people a gut feeling there was something unusual about the economy. In many ways, the mood since has matched that of the Great Depression:

- Economists, politicians, and the media argued that the deficit-strained economy couldn't sustain growth and technical progress unless the roles of business, unions, and government changed.
- With major trading partners suffering the same economic malaise, world trade relations fell into disarray, threatening protectionism.
- Economic woes prompted new social movements (e.g., Ross Perot's *United We Stand* in America and Preston Manning's *Reform Party* in Canada). They challenged the political orthodoxy, often with extreme and divisive views, and offered simplistic quick-fix solutions.
- Incumbent leaders either offered gradualism (George Bush) or said they'd curb the power of "elites" and "open up" the political system (Canada's Kim Campbell). Both got scant support from a dispirited and frustrated population seeking futuristic change.

Since the 1930s, little heed has been paid to the undoubted long-wave impact of technological change on the economy. For example, the automobile revolution peaked in 1962, and the machine-driven, oil-based economy collapsed with the

OPEC oil price shock of 1973. In an attempt to keep the economy going, over-expansion of money supply led to rampant inflation. The supposed cure, Ronald Reagan's supply side fallacy — a debt-binge of historic magnitude — created false prosperity and an economy which collapsed under its own debt load in 1989.

From 1989 to 1992, we witnessed nothing less than a modern-day depression. Forecast in my 1989 book *G-FORCES*, I labelled it a "Mini-Depression" only because social safety nets (created after the 1930s) and the avoidance of a glob-al trade war would prevent a full-blown depression *(see chart)*. The "Mini-Depression" marked another long-wave shift to a tele-computer-driven, info-based economy.

As the Info Economy takes off and the long-wave repeats, we will enjoy a sus-tained and hefty "Super-Boom" until about 2020, the next peak. In effect, the next 25 years will be a rerun of the post-WWII boom.

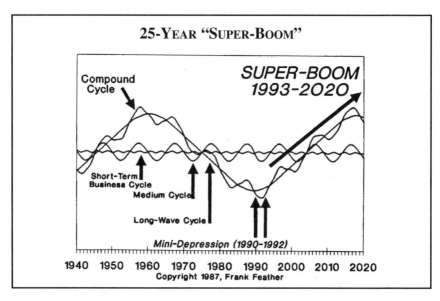

Economic/business cycles of various length occur simultaneously, forming a compound long-wave identified by Harvard University economist Joseph Schumpeter after the 1929 stockmarket crash. The last long-wave ran about 58 years, again ending with what Schumpeter called a period of "creative destruction." The stockmarket crashed in 1987, 58 years after 1929. The bot-tom of the Great Depression was 1933. Add 58 years and you get 1991, the bottom of the recent "Mini-Depression." The last long-wave peaked in 1962. Add 58 years and you get 2020 as the next peak. Hence, we can now expect 25 years of virtually uninterrupted prosperity.

Where will the wealth come from? There are three sources:
- Tele-computer productivity gains;
- Global free trade;
- Domestic savings and investment.

Tele-Computer Productivity Gains

At its root, economic growth is driven by technical innovation. Innovation spawns real productivity gains which then boost real wealth. With continued innovation, an economy's value can expand indefinitely. It's that simple.

This time through the upswing of the long-wave, we will be using technology of such profound economic impact that new wealth-creation will be unprecedented. In truth, we don't yet know the limits of info-technology. For sure, we're experiencing a veritable info-explosion, accompanied by dramatic boosts in computing power to deal with it. Best of all, computer cost-performance ratios are improving by 20%-30% per year. As costs plummet and processing speeds accelerate, tele-computers will have multiplier effects on productivity and economic output.

This will not be without precedent. During the last three long-waves, productivity growth rates were much weaker in the "depression decades" of the 1880s, 1930s, and 1980s. It took industry two decades to reap the benefits of investments in electricity that led us out of the depression of the 1880s. Firms spent heavily on electric motors in the 1890s, yet productivity didn't take off until after WWI in the 1910s. Similarly, Henry Ford invented the production line in the 1910s, and it was imp-roved in the 1920s and 1930s. But modern production lines didn't come into widespread use until after the Great Depression and WWII, fueling the boom of the 1950s and 1960s.

The investment in robots and computers during the 1970s and 1980s is now fueling new productivity gains in the 1990s. An MIT study by Erik Brynjolfsson finds that the largest manufacturing and service companies realized an average return on info-tech investment of 81% a year between 1987 and 1991 — this at the depth of the "Mini-Depression."

The tele-computer revolution is also a worldwide phenomenon. Hence, there now will be exponential growth in both global and local markets, bringing record prosperity across the planet.

Global Free Trade

Economic growth also will be boosted by the rapid evolution of global free trade. In a *Global Village* marketplace, economic interdependence and integration across national and regional borders makes global free trade inevitable. History shows that, beyond the fear of economic domination by stronger trade partners, mutual benefits always evolve to spur economic growth. As planet-wide free trade emerges over the next decade or so, the global economic pie will grow exponentially.

Free trade pacts such as the General Agreement on Tariffs and Trade (GATT), the Asia Pacific Economic Cooperation (APEC) forum, and North America's NAFTA exemplify this "glocal" trend. A growing Mexican middle class will create new markets and investment opportunities for America and Canada. As Mexico's economy expands, its growing purchasing power will drive the entire "AMEXICANA" economy into a higher orbit, influencing local market growth.

As NAFTA takes off, the fastest growth in North America will occur along the "borderlands" of "AMEXICANA" *(see map, below),* especially in the major metro areas. Mexican trade will boost California and Texas, with the Dallas/Ft. Worth area growing dramatically. Canada-U.S. trade especially will boost the economies of Ontario, British Columbia, and Washington State, particularly in Toronto, Vancouver, and Seattle/Tacoma (Sea-Tac). Further trade pacts with Latin America will boost Florida and Georgia, especially in the Atlanta-Tampa region.

Finally, Pacific trade via APEC will further boost the entire Sea-Tac/Vancouver market, with this area coming to outrank Los Angeles within two decades.

Domestic Savings and Investment

Growth also will be spurred by stronger economic fundamentals. The process of "creative destruction" has wrung inflation out of the economy, and it will stay in the 2%-3% range during

"AMEXICANA" BORDERLAND MARKETS

Borderland Markets
Mega-Metros

SEA-TAC-VAN

CHI-DET-TOR-MONT

BOSTON-NY-WASH

LA-SAN DIEGO

DALLAS/ Ft.WORTH

ATLANTA-TAMPA

MEXICO CITY

the upswing. Despite the debt overhang, interest rates will stay attractive to those who need to borrow to invest.

However, the days of reckless borrowing are over for a while. Sobered by the "Mini-Depression," as in the late-1930s governments, companies and consumers are paying down debt and focusing on savings. There is a distinct switch from credit-based living to saving for the future.

Nearly 40 million debit/prepaid cards have been issued and their acceptance is growing rapidly. Transaction volume is expected to top $50 billion by the year 2000, up from $12 billion in 1993. Gas stations, supermarkets, and convenience stores now accept debit cards, prompting banks and automated teller machine (ATM) networks to promote them to customers. **Visa**'s *Interlink* program just signed up 10,000 **Exxon** gas stations, and **MasterCard** is testing its *Maestro* debit card in postal service locations and fast-food stores. **Ameritech** now issues prepaid cards worth $2, $5, $10, or $20 for use in making phone calls.

These trends mark a search for a more sustainable lifestyle in a public issues-driven society.

4. Issues-Driven Politics

Hence, the fourth major force changing the marketplace is the need to strike a sustainable economic balance through more responsible living. The age of blatant party politics is over; we've entered the age of bipartisan issues politics — and the age of issues marketing.

In the future, ideological parties will still exist. But, as shown by recent election results, issues can span the entire political spectrum. The party which best addresses major public concerns — regardless of ideology — will gain most public support. It will be the same for business.

Let's review the major social responsibility issues of the next decade under three main headings:

- Sustainable Economics
- Environmentalism
- Other "Hot" Issues

Sustainable Economics

The budget deficit issue revolves around the traditional ideological split over how to create and distribute wealth. In the info-based, tele-computer era, socialist and capitalist thinking will converge. Consider the following:

- **Information** is the new factor of production. It is the instigator of innovation (a wealth creator), and, in the Information Age, we are about to create abundant wealth with minimum use of capital and labor.

• **Tele-computers** are social levelers (wealth distributors). They empower people with immediate access to information (i.e., the new form of wealth) from diverse sources, hence assuring wealth distribution.

Hence, the old debate about *"tax and spend"* or *"borrow and spend"* misses the point. Productivity gains are the only way to create real wealth or pay down debt.

A related but equally irrelevant ideological dispute is whether to run the economy with a central plan or allow market forces to dictate its progress. Tele-computerized info lets you do both: you can centralize *and* decentralize economic activity and coordination.

Socialism, recognizing the inefficiency of central planning, is adopting local market mechanisms to create wealth. Capitalism, always renewed by market freedom, still suffers the social costs of free-for-all competition that can impede progress. It must become more socialistic if sustainable economic progress is to be achieved. During the next long-wave, both ideologies will dissolve into a "mixed" hybrid of *socialistic capitalism* or, as in China, *market socialism*.

China's "one country, two systems" model is building a *"socialist market"* economy. This hybrid model, as explained in *China Vision*, an upcoming book written with my Chinese wife Tammie Tan, has spurred sustained GNP growth of 10% a year since 1979 — a performance without precedence by any country in history.

America periodically practices socialistic capitalism. In *America Born & Reborn*, Harvey Wasserman observed political cycles which parallel the economic long-wave, each starting with a burst of energy and carrying into a social "awakening." In *Cycles of American History*, Arthur Schlesinger described a cycle that swings between public purpose and private interest. Similarly, in *Populism and Elitism*, Jeffrey Bell defined a cycle between elitism and populism, where populists focus on public issues and candidates who represent their special interests.

Americans *are* increasingly concerned with idealistic issues of all kinds. With the Cold War over (if only temporarily), the 1992 election saw people respond to Bill Clinton's "new covenant." America is always rich in new ideas, and the virtue of sustainability (socioeconomic and ecological) will be the next ticket to renewed affluence and purpose.

The late 1990s promise to bring the society John Kennedy gave us a brief glimpse of before he was taken from us and the last long-wave peaked out. As people coalesce around the Clinton/Gore futuristic platform and the "Super-Boom" takes off, a whole new surge of optimism will arise, growing strongly toward 2000 and lasting well into the new millennium.

Environmentalism

A big part of this optimism will be based on environmental progress. Ecology is no fad. It is a widespread glocal issue, from global worries about the ozone layer to local concerns about waste disposal. The *Global Village* simply demands "high-virtue" business approaches to preserve a liveable ecosystem.

In 1992, the UN's *Earth Summit* gave renewed impetus to these concerns. The U.S. presidential campaign, with ecology advocate Al Gore on the Democratic Party ticket, reinforced the priority of environmental preservation and sustainable economic practice. Thus, although the "Big Green" initiative was defeated in California, it will come back in the form of "Little Greens" across the continent.

Already, more than 600 companies have signed up to voluntarily reduce emissions of 17 different toxic substances under the EPA's *"33/50"* program. And the Clean Air Act requires that auto fleets in more than 20 urban regions operate "clean fuel vehicles" (CFVs) that use methanol or natural gas. By 1998, 30% of fleet purchases in these areas must be CFVs, and the ratio jumps to 50% in 1999 and to 70% by 2001. In California, 2% of new vehicle sales must be "zero emission" by 1998, rising to 5% by 2000 and 10% by 2003. The auto industry is racing to comply.

Globally, the International Standards Organization (ISO), whose new *ISO 9000* series of standards encourage excellence in everything from design to quality control, is developing other standards that promote environmentally sound manufacturing and products. Companies that meet the standard will be able to label their products accordingly.

Other "Hot" Issues

In addition to economic sustainability and ecology, other top priority issues for consumers include:

- jobs (and "worksharing");
- education/retraining;
- healthcare;
- eldercare;
- abuse (of women/children);
- substance abuse (drugs/alcohol/tobacco);
- crime; and
- urban rehabilitation.

While none of these need further elaboration, the public mood is clearly changing, and customer behavior will mirror the changes.

That's the subject of the next section.

Checklist for "Glocal" Marketers

Social Outcomes/Implications
- ✓ Understand and study the socio-cultural divergence of your customer base and how it is changing due to NAFTA and other *Global Village* forces.
- ✓ Stop buying generic demographic market research and zip code analyses.

Technical Outcomes/Implications
- ✓ The *Info Superhighway* is the virtual business arena.
- ✓ The *Electronic Cottage* is the virtual shopping mall.
- ✓ The *TeleCom Wallet* is the consumer's virtual purse.
- ✓ Informationalize or die!

Economic Outcomes/Implications
- ✓ In a world of electronic commerce, information is money.
- ✓ That was no recession! It was a "Mini-Depression" which marked the "creative-destruction" shift to an Info Economy.
- ✓ The world economy has entered an unprecedented 25-year "Super-Boom."
- ✓ Invest heavily in info-movement/management systems.
- ✓ Grasp the opportunities of NAFTA and other global free trade agreements.

Political Outcomes/Implications
- ✓ The business climate is "issues-driven."
- ✓ Focus on sustainable long-term viability, environmentalism, and other "hot" issues.

PREDICT CONSUMER BEHAVIOR

*Stop thinking about ethnic marketing as peripheral and
start thinking about it as the core business.*

—Jeff Campbell, Marketing VP, **Pepsi-Cola**

People are molded by forces at play in the world around them. Hence, based on the trends forecast in Step One, future consumer behavior is somewhat predictable. The main consumer dynamics of the new marketplace are:

1. Culture-Based Behavior
2. Techno-Sophistication
3. Value-Based Buying
4. Virtuous Lifestyles

1. Culture-Based Behavior

Personality is determined by ethnic origin (root culture) and the milieu in which people are born, raised, and become mature.

Marketers thus must study more than demographics and lifestyle psychographics. People may have common psychological drives, but their motivations are shaped by cultural and social heritage above all. Marketers thus must first consider *ethno*graphics and *bio*graphics, plus intangibles such as how people "bond" with their societal peers.

At Glocal Marketing Incorporated, we draw on cultural anthropology and social psychiatry to reveal how root culture as well as cross-cultural and cross-generational interplay affect buyer behavior. We study people in their natural state, both in their home surroundings and in society at large.

Our findings? People of different cultures simply lead different lifestyles and want different products to match.

Most products remain culture-bound for several generations. Everyday household items are the clearest example, the most obvious of which is food. A glance into any shopping cart at a supermarket checkout reveals where people come from and what's driving them. Indeed, the best way to discover a person's ancestry — and resultant buying behavior — is to look inside their kitchen cupboards or study the artifacts decorating their recreation room walls.

Marketing must consider root culture and the cultural milieu in which people are raised. We'll begin with root culture.

Root Culture

As seen and heard on hourly newscasts, people the world over are reasserting their ethnic identity. The "implosive" effect of the *Global Village* is causing exactly what Marshall McLuhan forecast: "retribalization" of all societies, including ours.

As North America becomes a multicultural mosaic, this reinforces the individual need to identify closely with root culture and triggers similar feelings among others. Non-Caucasian immigrants do not adopt North America's dominant European-based culture because it is simply alien to them. Rather, they stick strongly to their own.

Due to the faster growth of the Hispanic/Latino segment, its culture soon will influence our lives. Its beat will transform pop music (as has African-American); its food will enter our kitchens; Spanish will be common at school. Spanish-English bilingual signs and forms, already as common in America as are the French-English variety in Canada, will proliferate.

Southeast Asian-Americans do settle down faster, and they are more entrepreneurial than other ethnic groups. Their values also are similar to those of traditional European immigrants. But these values — close family, hard work, high savings, and solid education — are typically Confucian. Even a Hong Kong immigrant's root culture is predominantly Confucian, several generations of British colonialism notwithstanding.

Even among traditional European groups, ethnic differences of all kinds are evident. British immigrants are price-conscious but more credit-oriented than Italians. French or Greek people dislike credit but are more brand loyal. Even subethnic differences are important. Italians, for example, come from three main regions of Italy — north (Roman); center (Bergamo); south (Sicilian) — each with its own dialect, food, and customs.

Root culture is now the primary marketing issue, whether in Albuquerque, the Bronx, Quebec, or remote rural areas. Black and white alike are harking back to their roots; most Hispanics/Latinos never lost theirs. North America is now a multiethnic, culture-driven market. Future consumers will increasingly respond to their glocal cultural drives, rejecting almost any product that's insensitive to culture. Interracial marriage also complicates the ability to market to households; such efforts must account for more than one cultural influence.

Still, in a *Global Village*, all consumers are simultaneously part of both global culture and local community culture. This influences the way we feel about each other, smashes myths, changes perceptions, and exposes us to other values. Cultural diversity also brings an intense mixing of consumer tastes.

Forces similar to those that slowly blurred the identity of European ethnic groups may now be at work for new immigrants. But their mixing is not "melting pot" homogenization; it is "glocalization." And, while product taste is slowly "glocalizing," even food must meet cultural expectations.

Good examples are **Unilever**'s 85 flavors of chicken soup for the European market alone and **Campbell**'s 22-line soup range to satisfy American taste buds. **Kraft General Foods** also offers different formulations of its cheese slices to satisfy the dominant cheese preference in each national market. In future *(as we'll see in Step Five)*, such products need tailoring to local nuances *within* national markets — even in North America.

Yes, customers will increasingly try, and then partially adopt, once "foreign" products and services. But they will "mix and match" their lifestyles, picking discrete cultural pieces and merging them into a custom-tailored glocal whole.

Local shopping malls, for example, often provide a courtyard of fast foods invented by ethnic groups that may not even exist in the local neighborhood. This allows a single consumer to "belong" to any ethnic segment, at least temporarily.

Similarly, the National Restaurant Association reports that ethnic dishes now make up about 30% of restaurant entrées. Most folks have tried French, Italian, Mexican, and Chinese cuisine. Half of us have sampled Spanish, German, Greek, Japanese, and Latin-American dishes. Up to 10% have tried menus as diverse as Indian, Caribbean, Mid-Eastern, Korean, Thai, Vietnamese, Filipino, Russian, and African.

However, occasionally eating French food — even ordering in French from a French menu in a French restaurant — doesn't make you French. When people are at home, of course, they usually eat the food of their own culture and almost always speak their mother tongue. For example, studies show that 83% of Hispanic/Latin-Americans say they exclusively speak Spanish at home. Moreover, 77% say they are "Hispanic first, American second," 19% say they are equally Hispanic and American, and a mere 4% say they are "American first."

Hence, behavior can be either own-culture or other-culture specific. It's a matter of moment-to-moment personal choice, with people increasingly asserting their own identity. They simply expect to be recognized for who they are; they want personal, "high-touch," culture-sensitive service.

Cultural Milieu

Generations also exhibit distinct "cultural" traits. As noted in Step One, each generation bears a strong imprint of the milieu into which it is born and raised, plus some carry-over effects from prior generations or previous social milieu.

Each generation shares a collegial identity and a collective mind-set that governs its behavior. In turn, each generation believes its experience is the norm for everyone, and we expect others to behave like us. Every society has felt this "generation gap" for centuries.

The social milieu changes with the mood of the times, each long-wave cycle bringing a repetition of three generations:

Repressed Conformists	Overconfident Idealists	Angry Reactives
(birth years)	(birth years)	(birth years)
1877-1893	1894-1910	1911-1928
1929-1945	1946-1964	1965-1982
1983-2000	2001-2018	2019-2036

• **During an economic crisis** (1880s, 1930s, and the recent "Mini-Depression") angry reactives, now adults, raise a group of conformists who, in turn, rebuild technology and political institutions.

• **During a period of confidence** (early 1900s, 1950s, and the coming "Super-Boom") repressed conformist adults raise overconfident idealists who, in turn, redefine social values and economic culture.

• **During a socioeconomic malaise** (1910s, 1970s) overconfident idealist adults raise another generation of angry reactives who (often called a "lost generation") suffer the excesses of their often neglectful predecessors.

The long-wave thus affects everything from the nurture we receive in childhood to the nurture we give. Changing times influence us to raise our children in the opposite fashion of our own upbringing. Overprotected parents underprotect their children who later overprotect their own offspring. Parental attitudes also are deeply shaped by traditional ethnic values.

Each generation becomes so "brainwashed" by its own sociocultural milieu that it thinks its experience is the norm for everyone. We expect other generations to behave like us and don't understand why others turn out differently. And yet their similarly conditioned personalities simply won't allow them to be other than who they are. Hence, each new generation is "counterculture" to the previous one, and, for marketing purposes, each should be treated as a separate culture.

Looking toward the year 2004, the relevant marketplace generations, already identified in Step One, are as follows:

- "By-the-Book" Angry Reactives
- "By-the-Clock" Repressed Conformists
- "Baby Boom" Overconfident Idealists
- "Generation X" Angry Reactives
- "Real-Time" Repressed Conformists

"By-the-Book" Angry Reactives (born 1911-28)

Born during WWI and the prohibition era, this generation was raised in obedience and tradition but witnessed the excesses of the "Roaring '20s" and the resultant Great Depression. They also had to fight WWII. Good by-the-book "boy scouts," they firmly believe in social discipline and that history should move in orderly straight lines.

Past-oriented and resistant to change, they prolong old battles (the Cold War) and preside over the long-wave's eventual decline. During the last downwave (1964-91), the U.S. presidency was held exclusively by men of this generation.

As of 1994, this generation ranges in age from 66 to 83 and will gradually fade from the scene as we enter the 21st century.

"By-the-Clock" Repressed Conformists (born 1929-45)

The Great Depression/WWII crisis meant overprotection for children. Parents demanded perfection in everything from fast toilet training to early weaning. Their children developed a compulsive obsession with detail, neatness, punctuality, time overscheduling, and unrealistic self-expectations. Clock-watchers, they believe in the work ethic, loyalty, and the importance of hierarchy.

Influenced by the hardships they and their parents overcame in the Great Depression and WWII, they focus on today's needs. They see work as the purpose of life — an end in itself — and gain their identity from it.

As of 1994, this "organizational man" generation is 49-65 years old and, having obsessively spearheaded "quality control" in the 1980s, has begun sliding into retirement. By 2004, even its youngest members will be in their 60th year.

As people seek an easier life, extra product features will have less appeal than ease of use, comfort, and security. These concerns will appear not only in the demand for easy-to-use high-tech products, but in apparel, furnishings, cars, and travel. Functionality is also a key feature. Products must address their day-to-day needs. Older shoppers are less interested in how the product looks or the status it brings. They place higher value on ease of operation, comfort, efficiency, and practicality.

After the "Mini-Depression," security concerns extend way beyond fancy burglar alarms. Investments must be less risky, savings are more important than borrowing, and the retirement nest egg becomes an active concern. Clearly, risk reduction has a strong influence on aging customers, and they will respond to brand names, warranties, and liberal product return policies. Seeking reliability, they tend to purchase quality items.

"Baby Boom" Overconfident Idealists (born 1946-64)

Nurtured in the post-WWII era of confidence, and coming of age during the 1960s social awakening, "Baby Boomers" are future-oriented, new-age idealists in the traditional mold. Others regard them for their lofty values and creative energy.

Reared in a time of high family mobility, divorce, and the TV era, their values are heavily influenced by the mass media. Having grown up in relative comfort and prosperity, for them work is to support life — a means to an end. Believing they possess a unique transcendent view, self-immersed "Baby Boomers" firmly believe in their own values. Raised in the Space Age, many were the "spaced-out" flower-child "hippies" and war protesters.

Yet, gaining full power by electing Bill Clinton in 1992, this generation will totally transform society as it ages into the next century. By 2004, the "Baby Boom" generation will be 40-58 years old. As people age, their values change; they "bloom" into maturity. Just as caterpillars become butterflies, "Boomers" are "morphing" into "Baby Bloomers." They are stretching their wings, broadening their cultural horizons, and experiencing a brand-new world.

Their individualism is not selfishness — at least not for most of them — but a matter of personal style. To realize their full potential, the 1960s taught them that value must be assigned to caring, sharing, harmony with nature, and ethical community behavior. They simply want to make a personal statement within acceptable community norms which, for them, are glocal.

Middle-aging people are primarily concerned with health, comfort, and future well-being. A desire to prolong life shows itself in fitness, nutrition, and environmental trends. However, fitness itself is becoming middle-aged: jogging will slow to a walk while golf becomes very popular. You'll see less drastic dieting but more healthy eating, with more attention to labels, freshness, and ingredients. There will be more demand for natural foods and "earth-friendly" products.

Still, so many conflicting "expert" health claims came out in the 1980s that cynical consumers are heading back to "good taste." Super-premium ice cream and fast food are more popular than ever while high-nutrition, low-fat foods and fat/sugar substitutes get lip service. People order a tofu burger for lunch but eat a *Snickers* bar for an afternoon snack. Food is a source of solace during times of midlife stress. Sales of ice cream, chocolate, and popcorn are each growing by 9% a year.

It also goes without saying that mid-agers relocate less often, leading to less purchasing of durables, less start-up housing spending, and less discretionary money going on basics. Rather they turn toward intangible acquisitions, like experiences and learning, and take pleasure in helping others. As they seek out leisurely "home-away-from-home" experiences, the travel and hospitality industry will boom.

"Generation X" Angry Reactives (born 1965-82)

They came of age amid the OPEC oil crisis and hyperinflation of the 1970s. Experiencing the "Mini-Depression" and resultant widespread unemployment, angry "Generation Xers" desperately seek to escape or outwit the judgments of the idealist "Baby Boomers" in whose shadow they live.

Today's rebellious misfits — also called *"Generation X"* and the *"Baby Bust"* generation — had to grow up fast in the face of parental self-immersion or even neglect. The generation many women took pills *not* to have, half of them also suffered a messy divorce, parental remarriage, and *"Brady Bunch"*-like family realignments. During the 1970s, the number of "latch-key" kids (alone at home after school) roughly doubled. Baby-sat by the TV, they cynically disparage career "Baby Boomers" by, for example, calling an office cubicle a *"veal fattening pen."* The children of AIDS, economic malaise, and violence, they are intolerant of these problems and want to solve them.

This group clearly is counterculture to the dominant one before, and, in their economic vulnerability, they share another common alienation. Also reared during Watergate and other scandals, they feel cheated out of the American dream. Realizing they bear the burden for Reagan's debt-based false prosperity, they are working younger, longer, later at night, and at more dangerous jobs. Two-thirds believe they will have to work harder than earlier generations simply to enjoy the same living standard.

Unlike the "Baby Boomers," the "Generation Xers" also come from myriad subgroups and ethnic minicultures, each thinking its own thoughts and listening to its own music. Exposed to the *"Global Village,"* they more readily accept differences in race, family structure, and lifestyle. They practice something called *"ethnomagnetism,"* or living in *"emotionally demonstrative"* ethnic neighborhoods.

Past-oriented and searching for stability amidst a dizzying sea of change, they pursue a lifestyle of "decade blending." In clothing, they indiscriminately combine two or more items from various decades to create a personal mood with a "retro" look. Today's modern woman combines *Mary Quant* earrings (from the 1960s) with cork wedgie platform shoes (1970s) and black leather jacket (1950s and 1980s). This generation also likes a "cool" environment of teak furniture (1950s), cut flowers (1960s), black-and-white art (1970s), and black matte high-tech items (1980s).

While they were often seen in shopping malls during their teens, they also reject mallism (*"malls have no exterior"*) but adopt them into their lifestyle: a kitchen is a *Food Fair*, a living room a *Fun Center*, the bathroom the *Water Park*.

When they shop, they often practice *"emallgration,"* going to low-tech, low-info environments with less emphasis on consumerism. Still, inspired by Madonna's "material" world, they buy cosmetics, clothing, and "fun stuff" such as computers, TVs, and stereos. But they also practice *"conspicuous minimalism"* or the nonownership of any product previously flaunted as a token of moral and intellectual superiority. For them, *"purchased experiences don't count,"* and, faced with unlimited choice, they tend to make none.

"Real-Time" Repressed Conformists (born 1983-2000)

Nurtured amid the trauma of the "Mini-Depression" crisis, these "infonauts" believe themselves more powerful and realistic than older generations. Less materialistic, they're involved with rap music, fashion, social concerns, culture, and sports. Like the "Generation Xers," they like diverse colors in their wardrobe because they see no need to conform — yet!

Determined to have a career, dual wage-earner households will be the norm for this generation. Eating out, movies, sports — and delayed childbirth — will predominate. Later in life, having matured and succeeded during the "Super-Boom," we'll regard them as uniquely optimistic, collegial, disciplined, and competent. Like their "By-the-Clock" predecessors who built and drove along interstate highways, this "Real-Time" generation is already driving along the information superhighway!

Today's youth culture is the first true *Global Village* generation. Endlessly searching for and adopting novel ideas and things, they will tour the world incessantly — in person and electronically. Techno-leaders, they are more likely to use computers, cellphones, cable TV, and video games. What's more, by the late 1990s, the eventual tele-computer "Class of 2000+" will already be the virtual-reality crowd.

2. Techno-Sophistication

Rapid electronic and other technical advances are making all products — and all buyers — more sophisticated as knowledge and information equalize quickly across society. This shared experience is leading to rapid innovation, shorter product life cycles, and rapid cycle response. It also equalizes product quality and refocuses customers on other product elements, especially the custom-tailored aspects. More and more people are techno-sophisticates, living in an "instant-on" society and often tele-commuting to work and almost anyplace else.

"Instant-On" Society

People increasingly expect real-time service delivery and sophisticated product utility. Even the "By-the-Clock" generation graduated from slide rules to calculators to computers, and from typewriters to word processors. Later generations grew up in a push-button world of instant-on TV, remote controls, banking machines, fax machines, microwave meals, drive-throughs, fast pizza delivery, jet planes, and cellphones. We simply expect instant access and fast service — anyplace, anytime.

With computer connected to satellite, we are tele-nomads, searching the *Global Village* for informational nourishment. We are "info hunters and gatherers."

"Baby Bloomers," weaned on TV and banking machines, have been trained from birth to demand instantaneous "telepresent" attention — which their multimedia telecomputer terminals and *TeleCom Wallets* will make possible. For them, technology is a metaphor for reshaping life and work.

Tele-commuters

Already about 48 million North Americans now work at or from home. The number of tele-commuting employees grew 20% in 1993 to 10 million, and the total number of tele-commuters (including freelancers) is expected to top 53 million by 1996. While only 7% put in at least 35 hours per week at home, the average is 17 hours per week and increasing.

The share of homeworkers with a PC rose from 35% in 1988 to 56% in 1993. Moreover, *American Demographics* magazine reports that, for 11% of Americans, a PC now rivals the phone in importance and has become a "life necessity." More than 20% of affluent adults consider PCs essential, and 25% of college graduates say they couldn't live without one.

The young "Real-Time" generation of infonauts could afford and use a calculator in first grade (unless they had a change-resistant "By-the-Clock" teacher who refused to allow it). They accept and expect technology to be part and parcel of their lives. Already cruising the info superhighway, they will be the principal consumers of computer-designed and computer-delivered products and services and the main users of interactive networks.

As our "keyboard culture" grows, interactive multimedia services will predominate the retail environment. More people are becoming dependent on electronic access to products, services, and entertainment.

In this real-time environment, modern telecom systems are vital to effective market competition. Time and convenience are already key factors, and companies must deliver products and services at top speed and in the most techno-sophisticated way. Time is the most precious currency of today's consumer. During the "Super-Boom," with lots of discretionary money but little time, people will happily trade one for the other. While this has to be good news for service and convenience industries, people will spend their money carefully.

3. Value-Based Buying

Traditionally, as indicated, volatile swings in economic activity cause parallel swings in consumer behavior. In the past, those who experienced the depressions of the 1880s and 1930s were traumatized into frugality. They "saved for a rainy day," delaying purchases and shunning credit.

We've seen a similar mood emerge during the recent "Mini-Depression," triggering another bout of frugality and a search for value. Enlightened buyers are switching from spending to saving and seek value through solid information.

Switch From Spending to Saving

The "excessive 1980s" of "buy now, pay later" have given way to the "nervous

1990s" of "become debt free." Indeed, three out of four customers say they will never return to their old spending ways. Aging "Baby Boomers" — now worried about the looming cost of their kid's education, healthcare for themselves and their aging parents, plus their own retirement costs — are switching from credit-based consumption to saving. They want to pay for things ahead of time out of savings, not later out of earnings. As a result, prepaid cards and/or so-called "debit" cards will outnumber credit cards within a decade.

Hence, although the resurgent affluence of the coming "Super-Boom" will boost confidence and spending power, consumers will keep frugal habits. While their savings will generate record business investment and personal spending during the next 25 years, consumers will not buy at *any* price.

Enlightened Buying

Even affluent consumers want to preserve the gains they have made in life. Cautious about quick money gains in the 1980s and looking to preserve their wealthy status in the 1990s, affluent values have turned traditional. Quality and value will be the main concern of affluent buyers as they shift from "conspicuous" to "enlightened" consumption.

Following their lead, the mass market also has turned toward smart values — quality at a fair price, especially brand names. With the return to low inflation, price competition will intensify and all buyers will expect prices to "glocalize" across markets. Hence, high-value local product offerings are essential to global market success.

Today's consumers are professional shoppers: they justify every purchase and maximize the value of every dollar spent. They simply want top quality at the lowest possible price. Seeking "total value," they don't necessarily want "best in class" but "best in budget range."

Price-conscious consumers will pay more for products in which they have an ego investment. These bargain hunters are proud of themselves for being smart shoppers — for beating the system. They insist on the *Ralph Lauren* label but are willing to buy it from a factory outlet where the price is lower than in a boutique. Many are "cross-shoppers" who drive a *BMW* but pump their own gas and buy socks at **K Mart**.

Info-Based Value

This search for value is best satisfied by communicating info about products/services. Value is created when buyers access info in ways which create special meaning from it and somehow improve the buying experience. With information now the main value-creator in the economy, buyers will increasingly insist on making better-informed decisions.

Smart consumers simply expect to be fully informed about the product — as well as its personal *and* social benefits. This forces companies to create knowledge and make decisions close to the customer. Ads and packages, for example, must provide the detailed product info that sophisticated buyers demand. Buyers want products which not only perform but "inform" — and meet their new ideals about value: on labels, in brochures, and in advertising.

Glocal marketers also need to involve customers more and more in product design and development. Buyers expect to be listened to — and heard — on their ideas about products. They must be "plugged in" to the company; provided with easy and convenient access to real-time communication links with product and service providers, either through 800/900 numbers or computer bulletin board E-mail systems.

As will be discussed in Step Four, a real-time info-system is the only vehicle for delivering knowledge-based value to future consumers.

4. Virtuous Lifestyles

The 1990s also are a far cry from the often outright unethical business morals of the "excessive 1980s." Indeed, with the modern-day ecology movement having begun in the 1960s, many former "hippies" are now in corporate board rooms and executive suites. They are leading a movement back to virtuous capitalism with socially responsible business practices.

Virtuous Capitalism

People inside and outside business realize there is no trade-off between virtue and economic wealth. They are finding that more virtuous behavior brings greater economic rewards, not less. Even George Bush observed at the U.N. in 1991:

Economic growth and environmental integrity are not contradictory. One reinforces and complements the other.

Economic and environmental deficits are two sides of the same coin. Although techno-innovation is the key to their combined solution, it is not enough. To cure *both* deficits and renew economic health, sustainable production and consumption practices are essential.

Of course, U.S. ideology is largely based on individualism, free markets, and limited government. But these values became too dominant under Reagan, and his cavalier approach led to *laissez faire* gone mad. We got rampant speculation, corruption, manipulation, a debt binge of leveraged buyouts with "junk" bonds, the S&L debacle — and environmental disregard. More than anything, the monstrous budget deficit reveals the economic morality of the 1980s — an unwillingness to accept discipline and a slowness to respond to change.

Community Interests

Such crass commercial abandon yielded empty rewards to people seeking deeper meaning in their lives. Hence, they sought a sense of community through shared interests in specific issues, joining special interest groups. The way consumers relate to public issues (such as environmentalism, or crime, or anything else) has become a key component of their marketplace motivation and behavior. After the loud, greed-driven 1980s, consumers simply want a quieter, more ethical life, with a socially responsible focus.

Sobered by the "Mini-Depression," all consumers are more objective and will respond positively to *genuine* product value claims. They'll hunt for ethically sound ("high-virtue") products, buying from firms they see as mature, ethical, and socially responsible — like themselves.

Indeed, they are insisting that government, business, and society unite to restore sustainable prosperity. People want quality of life, not quantity of life. Marketers have no choice but to offer products and services which let us experience life to the fullest — but in harmony with local community values and the natural environment.

In particular, firms must adopt a "green" ethic throughout their operations and reflect this in all products and services. Otherwise, buyers will switch brands and even boycott products. Consumers simply want earth-friendly products that don't compromise on performance or value but which promote overall quality of life.

"Green" consumers will account for more than half the population by 2000. The majority (74%) already say they are more likely to buy a product whose packaging is degradable or recyclable, and 78% will pay extra for such packaging. Indeed, products in packaging which helps buyers cut down on solid waste, pollution, and degradation of nonrenewable resources are growing 30 times faster than all new packaged goods.

Consumers also will reward companies which work hard to be relevant on other "hot" social and community issues (such as crime) and who let consumers know that. To get on a consumer's list of "good" companies, firms must both offer relevant products and be a relevant offerer — that is, share buyer concerns and priorities and do something about them.

Many companies are skating on thin ice with consumers. All firms, as well as their products and market presentation, must be "issue-relevant" to be customer-relevant. Through ethical, virtuous behavior, business can and must play its role in restoring a sustainable society. It's that simple.

Checklist for "Glocal" Marketers

With four major groups of forces changing customer behavior, you need to respond to four sets of outcomes/implications:

Social Outcomes/Implications
✓ Understand that the behavior of consumers (and of employees and suppliers) is predetermined by root culture and the social milieu in which people were raised.
✓ Realize that there is much more to the market than the "Baby Boom" generation.
✓ Respond to individualized expectations with "high-touch," individually tailored, culture-oriented products.
✓ Help people "mix and match" their lifestyles.

Technical Outcomes/Implications
✓ The functional utility of products should be "high-tech" but suit "high--touch" cultural nuances.
✓ People expect real-time delivery and anyplace/anytime access.
✓ Growing numbers of buyers expect to be able to shop for products/services from their *"Electronic Cottage"* at home.

Economic Outcomes/Implications
✓ Satisfy customers' continued frugal search for "high value" by providing info-intensive education about product benefits to help buyers make well-informed decisions.
✓ All products and services should offer "total" value (not just quality), the new prestige.

Political Outcomes/Implications
✓ Develop and offer products which are ecologically sound ("high-virtue") throughout the value chain.
✓ Consumers will increasingly respond favorably to companies which address other important social and local community issues in a customer-relevant way.

You must match each of these *high-touch, high-tech, high-value, high-virtue* dynamics with a progressive set of core competencies, discussed next in Step Three.

MASTER CORE COMPETENCIES

*We're becoming a "learning academy" that
shares, gathers, and networks knowledge,
turning it into a corporate value.*

—Roger Levien, VP Marketing, **Xerox**

The glocal marketing race is on. Firms that understand the new *Global Village* market and future customer behavior are rushing to develop matching core competencies.

Glocal marketing success demands quality *across* the firm — human, technical, informational, and ethical. Step Three discusses four glocal core competencies for the late 1990s and beyond:

> **1. Employee Empowerment** *(Intellectual Capital)*
> **2. Proprietary Products** *(Innovation Capital)*
> **3. Info-Intensity** *(Information Capital)*
> **4. Community Ethics** *(Ethical Capital)*

1. Employee Empowerment *(Intellectual Capital)*

Market winners know that the core strength of a competitive business comes first from its people — their values, skills, and autonomy. Glocal firms will use knowledge to empower *each* employee to play a role in the purchase process.

Some firms, after they install "smart" technology, try to replace "smart" workers with "dumb" ones. That's dumb! Information intensity changes the context of work and requires mastery of yet *higher* order skills among *all* employees.

Smarter people can handle greater info-complexity. Success starts with managers who help people deal with information as it enters the firm, before it flows across the system unfettered. When employees bog down in information, they stop learning. When info is managed at the point of contact with the marketplace, learning is accelerated.

Human quality stems from the development of intellectual capital and employee empowerment. Akio Morita, founder and chairman of **Sony**, explains it this way:
> *What is the secret formula behind the success of Japanese companies? It is very simple. The human infant is born curious, but natural curiosity drains away with age. It's my job to nurture the curiosity of the people I work with.*

*At **Sony**, we know that a terrific new idea is more likely to happen in an open, free, and trusting atmosphere.*

Such thinking is genuinely inspiring and empowering. Empowered people form a corporate culture that doesn't freeze in the face of change; rather it relishes the future. Self-confident people feel good about themselves and their customers; about their competence to satisfy diverse needs and exceed future customer expectations. They are better than customers expect because they share a corporate memory of glocal market knowledge. They tap a constantly changing "virtual image" of the glocal marketplace's fluid reality, or its "flow."

Human quality is best developed in a "learning" culture; one that arouses curiosity. People enjoy learning and take pride in their accomplishment. Learning is something you do for yourself. Skills cannot be "taught," or "trained" into people. Training is for animals. Learning is for humans — and should be fun. After all, *humor* derives from the word *human*.

Hence, skills acquisition must be learner-based, with people guiding their own development through individually-tailored lessons. The learning center should be on-site — just like the company library, exercise room, daycare center, or cafeteria — and it can be a "virtual" resource center using telecom links.

For example, **American Bankers Association** uses its *American Financial Skylink* satellite TV network to deliver 2 hours per week of bank-specific training, financial news, and other info exclusively for bankers. In Canada, **Stentor** has begun the first fully digital Voice on Demand (VOD) trial in Ottawa at the capital's two universities. Students and faculty access libraries of video programs stored at a remote location, including taped course lectures and film clips. They are viewed through a PC, receiving the video signal via regular phone lines.

The learning center thus should provide menu-driven telecomputer access to self-learning modules which focus on the glocal market challenge, including at least four skills:
- "Glocal" Instinct
- Borderless Customer-Focused Teamwork
- Trans-Cultural Skills/Values
- Trans-Gender Skills/Values

"Glocal" Instinct

In the *Global Village*, it is critically important to manage ambiguity, complexity, and anomaly. As F. Scott Fitzgerald said:

The test of a first-rate intelligence is the ability to hold two opposed ideas in mind and still function.

There's no substitute for glocal instinct. By thinking globally and acting locally, people become globally objective and locally subjective. They intuitively see the world "glocally."

In essence, glocal employees mentally adopt the *nitoryu* skill of Musashi, a Japanese *samurai*. This is the art of handling two swords — one long, one short — and knowing which one to use. It's also like learning *metsuke*, a way of seeing as if with two sets of eyes. The Japanese call this *"a distanced view of close things."* Such glocal viewing is like adapting to bifocal eyeglasses — except more so.

Becoming a geo-strategic thinker, an employee's mind must be bifocal (global+local), bringing the *Global Village* anomaly into sharp focus. That's glocal instinct. To develop this mental skill, virtual reality and creativity workshops should be readily available to all employees.

Borderless Customer-Focused Teamwork

Such glocal employees will create a boundaryless customer space, which demands cross-functional people skills or teamwork. Indeed *(as detailed in Step Four)*, corporate functions must fuse into processes that focus on market needs. Companies need to regroup into networks woven around the marketing process, even abolishing separate functions such as RD&E (Research, Development, & Engineering), production, or finance. In any event, all must be secondary to marketing, subsumed by a glocal market focus.

Cross-functional teams create a customer-focused culture. In such a work environment, there are few barriers between employees, or between the firm, its vendors, and its customers. They become a full part of the team. For example, as well as educating its own people, **Rosenbluth Travel** explains the corporate travel business to clients. **Xerox** educates its suppliers' employees to assure a full understanding of customer demands. **Motorola** even educates the employees of its suppliers' suppliers!

These companies realize that being service-driven isn't enough to exceed customer expectations. A 1992 survey by McKinsey & Company found that 68% of all customers cite "indifference to their needs" as the main reason they don't come back. Being customer-driven is nothing new at **Johnson & Johnson**. The following set of strategic criteria has been in place at **J & J** since General Johnson formulated them in the 1920s:
- J & J's **first** responsibility is to our **customers**;
- J & J's **second** responsibility is to our **employees**;
- J & J's **third** responsibility is to our **community**;
- J & J's **last** responsibility is to our **shareholders**.

The same principle guides **Merck**, the pharmaceutical giant. First articulated in 1950 by son-of-founder George Merck, and repeated ever since, its credo runs: *Never forget, medicine is for people. It is not for profits. The profits follow and, if we remember that, they never fail to appear.*

Interestingly, the Japanese word for customer is *kokyaku*. This two-part word literally translates into *"To take personal care of ... honorable and respected guest"* — and market leaders do just that. **Nissan**, for example, invites potential *Infiniti* buyers to drop in for a *"Guest Drive."*

Similarly, **Marriott** has an *"Honored Guest Awards"* frequent travel program. The hotel chain also uses a *"ServQual"* weighted index to rate customer service quality:

• 30% — reliability *("we do what we say")*
• 25% — responsiveness *(helpfulness)*
• 20% — assurance *(trust)*
• 15% — empathy *(caring)*
• 10% — tangibles *(appearance, etc.)*

The aim of such programs is to get the customer to come back again. **Marriott** uses a video-based educational program of true-life situations to help employees (called associates) be extra responsive to guests. The company empowers people to *"remove barriers"* to customer service *"within the boundaries"* of business prudence. As CEO Bill Marriott observes:

Businesses succeed or fail one customer at a time. Treat them right and they'll keep coming back.

To generate repeat business, learning programs thus should directly link every employee to the glocal marketing goal. For example, to directly reward customer-conscious employees, **Big Cheese Pizza** gives a pay raise to waiters after they learn the names of 100 loyal customers. **Federal Express** employees learn to care about total customer satisfaction; they genuinely want you to use **FedEx** again and again. **Singapore Airlines** instills a commitment in *all* employees, not just flight attendants, *"to treat **each** passenger as an honored guest — so he/she will **want** to fly with us again."*

Trans-Cultural Skills/Values

A company's workforce should also mirror the increasingly culture-driven market. Thanks to immigration, North American firms are blessed with a *Global Village* pool of people skills to draw from. To tap this pool, a glocal company will adopt a "no frontiers" recruiting policy. It then can build a cosmopolitan workforce which reflects the diverse cultural aspirations of its customers.

Yes, **Singapore Airlines** would be even better with multicultural flight crews. Speaking English and being "Westernized" is no longer enough in serving "Western" passengers who now have glocal values. It's even less sufficient in serving people of other cultures, no matter how cosmopolitan they are.

Marketers must help multicultural consumers mix-and-match their cosmopolitan lifestyles, offering glocal products that meet a customer's individual *and* global ideals.

Nissan's advertisements thus feature a multicultural design team engineering cars *"for the human race."* Similarly, **Matsushita**'s creed is:
> *To promote the general welfare of society and devote ourselves to the further development of world culture.*

To develop trans-cultural values, firms should also provide glocal career paths. A career should be a market-focussed glocal network journey, not a head office pyramid-climbing expedition. And simply providing exposure to "foreign" cultures by assigning employees "abroad" is not enough. Unless they absorb themselves in learning to soak up the new culture, mono-cultured managers stay mono-cultural.

That's why Japanese companies decide "foreign" assignments at least a year before employees depart. During that year, the chosen employees learn the culture, customs, and way of doing business — plus the language — of the country to which they are going. Over time, these companies thus develop a mosaic of people skills embracing both language and culture.

Yes, English is the language of world business. However, mother tongue is passionately retained by *Global Village* consumers. Hence, the use of Spanish forges better ties in local Hispanic/Latino markets, in Mexico, most of Latin America, and Spain. And ability in French will magnify market share in Louisiana, Maine, New Hampshire, Vermont, Quebec, France, much of Africa, and Southeast Asian countries such as Vietnam.

Even more important than language is a knowledge of cultural nuances. The cultural skills of ethnic employees (especially Asians, Slavs, and Muslims) will forge valuable links to the dynamic Asia-Pacific market, East Europe, Russia, and across the Islamic world. Such cultural fluency would also boost market share in "Salad Bowl" North America!

Marketers that foster cultural interaction will be the most likely to succeed in the retribalized *Global Village*. The key lesson: Use your own "cultural" affiliations and those of your employees and associates to penetrate new markets.

And, should this contradict your notion of individualism and pluralism, remember that ethnic affiliation overshadows citizenship as a matter of personal identity.

Trans-Gender Skills/Values

Glocal companies also must be much more attuned to the trans-gender marketplace. Not only is one half of the market female, purchasing power has shifted dramatically. For example, as noted earlier, half the new cars in North America are owned or leased by women. Also, of course, most women drive, and they also drive more miles than men.

Astonishingly, most cars still don't have a vanity mirror built into the sun visor on the driver's side as basic equipment. Even men drivers would like a vanity mirror, so they can fix their hair and straighten their tie before walking in to an important meeting. Most car designers are macho men who still think it's the man's job to drive while the woman sits in the passenger seat. Notable exceptions are **Nissan**, which has one all-female design team, and **Ford**, where the best-selling *Taurus* was designed by a female-led team. The auto industry also has few women in dealer showrooms. Why?

It's the same story in most businesses. Though more than half of business school grads are women, their progress up the corporate hierarchy, though inevitable, is painfully slow. Of professionals and managers in the U.S. workforce, 47% are white males and 42% are women (the others are minorities). Yet only 7% of corporate directors and 6% of senior officers are female. Even the soap/cosmetic industry has only 17% female directors and a mere 4% female senior officers.

Still, there are grounds to expect faster progress. Despite their many shortcomings, business schools at least provide an atmosphere free of sexual stereotype where people learn to work together and complement each other's abilities. People find their careers enriched when they can work free of sex-role constraints. This best occurs through supra-sexual teamwork, a learnable skill which transcends gender to twin the unique intellectual abilities of both sexes.

Such skills spring from inborn complementary abilities of male and female brains. Biogenetically different, our brains are simply wired differently. Brain science shows that men and women don't use the same parts of their brains to perform the same task; they have different brain dexterity. Visual-spacial tasks (at which men are better) are done by the brain's right hemisphere; verbal tasks (at which women are better) are done on the left.

The two sides of a man's brain are unalike and highly structured, but a woman's is more symmetrical. She shifts back and forth between the two sides more easily. She's also more sensitive to context, good at picking up incidental information, and better at combining perceptual with verbal skills. Since the Information Age is built around info synthesis, women will be especially successful in this new era.

Men and women will never fully duplicate their innate brain differences. Hence, as the workplace is regrouped into teams and as women move into senior positions, firms must find ways to twin male-female brainpower. In creativity workshops, for example, we at Glocal Marketing Incorporated find that male-female teams consistently achieve 40% more-innovative results than same-sex teams. With supra-sexual "channeling," results can improve by 80% or more! Yet few companies are tapping this potent trans-gender skill in any significant way.

Glocal marketing is a holistic whole-brained process. Trans-gender brain power thus becomes vital to future success.

2. Proprietary Products *(Innovation Capital)*

Brain power is also critical to the second core competency, using continuous improvement to create proprietary products and build innovation capital through:
- "Core" Product Leadership
- Real-Time Borderless Telecom Networks
- Efficient Customer Response (ECR)
- "Virtual" Research

"Core" Product Leadership

A technological follower can never be a leader. Indeed, if you're only keeping up with technology, you've already fallen behind. In a fast-changing world, customer-driven product development, fast-cycle time, and rapid response, with continual, market-focused innovation, is crucial *(see box, below)*.

FOSTERING CONTINUOUS INNOVATION

Firms succeed in continuous innovation when they:
- **Understand** their customers;
- **Build upon** their core competencies;
- **Design** better business systems; and
- **Nurture** an innovative management state of mind.

Building on those strengths, firms can then:
- **Diagnose** their situation realistically;
- **Set** aspiration levels and a strategic focus;
- **Design** the facilitating organization structure;
- **Manage** the process with discipline; and
- **Maintain** a "restless" culture.

In terms of research and development (R&D), for example, most Japanese firms do "little r and big D." In contrast, we do "big R and little d." In the glocal marketing race, we need to be as innovative as **Sony**, which says R&D is RD&E (research, development, *and* engineering).

Indeed, glocal marketing starts *before* the RD&E phase. A "core" product shows a keen understanding of customer needs, matched by sharp technical abilities. Market winners thus develop "core" parts (or whole products) that customers want but cannot find — or have not yet even imagined their existence!

Technical "core" competencies shape local markets and build global brand share.

Indeed, because inside expertise cannot be emulated, a unique technical competency will lead to brand dominance. For example, **Canon**'s copier engine is now the unmatched "core" of photocopiers and laser printers worldwide. Similarly, **Intel** microchips and **Microsoft** software run most of the world's computers.

Thus, an irresistible function or inherent appeal makes a product unbeatable. It becomes the global *and* local standard for that product. Such core utility builds global brand equity by meeting local market needs. It is glocal. A portfolio of competencies (hardware, software, or expertise) often spawns the best proprietary products. For example:

• **Honda** developed world-class engines *(hardware)* for motorbikes and adapted this "core" technology to cars, lawn mowers, and marine engines worldwide.

• **Systems Center** markets a piece of computer network *software* (called *NET/MASTER*) which integrates computers made by different vendors. The key to success is the product's *Network Control Language* which is now a *de facto* network interface standard. This "core" technology has led the company into more than 50 countries and helped it develop other related products.

• **Boeing**'s *expertise* is that of an airplane wing specialist and systems integrator. It excels in aircraft design and assembly. The firm's *CATIA* design system, with 2,000 workstations, is the world's largest manufacturing sector computer network. The company also uses an *Integrated Aircraft Systems Lab* to build and test every airplane sub-system: flight controls, electronics, avionics, electric power, and propulsion. Before an airplane is even assembled, these systems function together in the lab in a "virtual" test flight.

"Core" technical competencies also change product mandating, where a local company has the sole mandate to make a product for the global market. It's becoming impossible to be globally competitive by making a full range of products in one local market. Product mandating is "glocalizing."

In a "glocalized" market, the main competition is *not* global but local. Hence, firms must make products that beat *local* standards of design, function, quality, and price. Local plants linked by a telecom network can become "mass customizers," making a global product to meet diverse local needs.

Northern Telecom, for example, used to design a variety of products for different country markets. In 1990, it began making items that plug into any electrical or phone outlet in any country, regardless of local voltage or pin standards.

Electronic networks — linking design, production, marketing, and customers — thus allow firms to concurrently engineer tailored products. This subjects new products to tough market scrutiny throughout the development cycle. Therefore, RD&E cannot be cloistered in the lab. It belongs to a quality marketing team that focuses on customer satisfaction.

To achieve this, **BICC Cables** set up a *Technology Council* linking the firm's global RD&E centers and creating an internal "know-bank." As chairman emeritus Harry Schell explains:

People are rotated between the centers to create team spirit, develop local market knowledge, and foster trans-cultural skills. It's the only way to gain a technological advantage, globally and locally.

Real-Time Borderless Telecom Networks

In the late 1990s, leading firms will also synergize "glocally dispersed" activities through real-time info-networks. The so-called multinationals sought a competitive edge via local access to cheap labor and resources. Today, all such industrial-era factors of production are transcended by the new glocal economic commodity, information.

In this new world, what the Japanese call Borderless Intelligent Manufacturing-Marketing Systems (BIMMS) will become the norm. Japanese companies are already installing BIMMS which span the globe. Using electronic data interchange (EDI), manufacturing is strategically located at local market leverage centers, *not* national supply bases. Such networking is a big change in how business is done. Control is decentralized to independent, market-driven, local units with their own RD&E, production, and marketing capability. Such local units:

• Pursue *local* content (as well as *global* sourcing), investing in *glocal* technology to assure quality of supply;

• Forge *global* alliances to gain flexible manufacturing ability and access *local* markets;

• Exploit the *local* market to generate *glocal* exports through the parent company's *global* distribution system.

Efficient Customer Response (ECR)

The traditional factory-driven model of marketing is based on forward buying of inventories at a discount and trade deals to "push" the product into the market. Meanwhile customer orders "pull" the product through the value chain. Hence, "push" meets "pull" in the distributor's warehouse, resulting in a build-up of inventory and inefficiency. This is because the product replenishment system is unlinked, as follows:

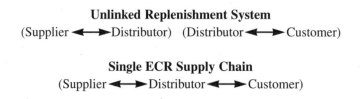

Unlinked Replenishment System
(Supplier ◄───► Distributor) (Distributor ◄───► Customer)

Single ECR Supply Chain
(Supplier ◄───► Distributor ◄───► Customer)

ECR integrates the replenishment loop at the distributorship into a single supply chain. The focus shifts from buying profitability (through "push" deals) to customer needs (through purchase "pull") and optimizes the two. Linking the value chain optimizes inventories and storage space and minimizes the time and cost involved in operating the system. More important, it links producers with consumers — what Alvin Toffler called a *"prosumer"* system — and speeds new product introductions.

In such a system, a distributor's warehouse becomes a true distribution center; a node in the logistics flow rather than a storage location. All three parties benefit, as follows:

- **Producer:** Reduced out-of-stocks; enhanced brand integrity; improved distributor relationship.
- **Distributor:** Increased customer loyalty; better customer knowledge; improved supplier relationships.
- **Consumer:** Increased choice and convenience; reduced out-of-stock items; latest/freshest product.

Early adopters of ECR will see increasing returns from their investments as more of their trading partners begin similar implementation. They will maintain their leadership by further-refining ECR and passing on extra cost savings to customers. As a result, they will grow much faster than competitors and will acquire weaker players as their industry consolidates.

McKesson, for example, became the world's largest pharmaceutical distributor by connecting U.S. and Canadian drug stores to its *Econolink-Pharmaserv* database ordering system. As soon as a pharmacist sends an order from an in-store terminal, a blue plastic shipping box slips onto a conveyor system in one of **McKesson's** three warehouses.

Bar-code scanners route it through an A-framed automatic order-picker. The computer triggers "flow racks" to toss drug packages into the blue box. Rarely-ordered items are taken from bar-coded shelves by people wearing computerized gloves with a point-and-click infrared scanner. A printer spits an itemized invoice into the shipping box and robots label/seal it and convey it onto a waiting truck. Orders are filled every five seconds, with 100% accuracy, and delivered overnight — something the drug firms themselves couldn't achieve. Simultaneously, new inventory is ordered from the manufacturers.

Connecticut Mutual improves client response through a data base which consolidates each customer's records. Via an enterprise-wide computer network architecture, workstations present data tailored to each job function. When a client calls, within seconds the service rep pulls up a complete profile, computes total cash value on her investments, and prints a consolidated statement — once a 2-3 week process. Death claims now take 4 days versus 21, and response to general queries is down from 5 days to 4 hours. As well, 20% fewer people are needed, and productivity is up 35%.

Walgreens drug store chain keeps a data base on the medications of individual customers. For the elderly, it even delivers single doses to the home so they can be taken at precisely the proper time. How's that for "mass-customized," "virtual" nursing?

"Virtual" Research

Virtual reality (VR) is increasingly being used to enhance corporate competency and improve market response.

Rolls-Royce, for example, is using VR to radically change aircraft engine design and maintenance evaluation procedures. Real engine mockups are very expensive, but potential maintenance problems show up during the fabrication process. Even modern CAD workstations don't provide an intuitive or natural view of the engine and its components. Using VR, however, designers can immerse themselves inside the engine to "experience" the planned layout of pipework, gearboxes, and brackets to assess their ease of servicing.

The **Cooperative Wholesale Society (CWS)**, Britain's [#]1 food retailer (also a travel agent, bank, and insurance company) believes VR is essential to maintaining its competitive edge. It uses VR to visualize shelf layouts and interact with space planners, product buyers, and supermarket managers. CWS also links VR with point-of-sale, electronic shelf-edge pricing and customer tracking systems to design, model, predict, and measure the performance of products and staff. It soon expects to offer the VR system for shopping itself.

To assist "infonauts," **Silicon Graphics**' *Info Navigator* lets you (as described in the *"Shopping in 2004"* scenario) "fly" over a 3-D "map" of bar-charted sales activity, just as you might hover above Manhattan skyscrapers in a helicopter. You can zero in to scrutinize up-to-the-minute details of which product is moving in which store; "skyscrapers" of fast-moving merchandise flash red on the screen.

Similarly, **Maxus Systems**' *Metaphor Mixer* is a VR stock portfolio which depicts different investment variables. You "swim" through a sea of data where corporate logos rise and fall with their stock value. Special opportunities and risks are highlighted as you hunt for the best investments.

Information is the source of all value; it is the capital of the Information Age.

3. Info-Intensity *(Information Capital)*

The third core competency is the creation of info-intensity. In the Information Age, *all* markets are electronic. Driven by information and operating in real time, they function through nodes of fast-spreading networks. Info-intensity adds value, builds information capital, and gains a glocal edge through:

- Info-Intensive Value Chain;
- Entrepreneurial Accountability; and
- "Glocal" Costing and Pricing.

Info-Intensive Value Chain

Info-intensity boosts company profit *and* market share. Indeed, both will always improve as technical competence is enhanced:

- **Old-fashioned, mechanized firms** boast of low labor and material costs. But such advantages are overwhelmed by technical innovation. U.S.-Canadian workers in automated plants are eight times as efficient as Mexican workers in nonautomated plants, so the large wage differential is offset. Firms that do not at least robotize and/or computerize simply will not survive into the next century.

- **Modern, robotized firms** broaden their sales and out-market purely mechanical ones. They also raise their marginal contribution to fixed costs, helping raise profit. But the mere automation of processes falls way short of the benefits which flow from sophisticated info management systems.

- **Info-networked firms beat them both.** They outpace nonautomated *and* automated competitors. Info-intensive firms achieve low fixed costs *and* low variable costs to create high value-added products. Such firms optimize both profit *and* market share. As with fast-food chains and bank branch network companies, they achieve local economies of scale *and* global economies of scope. Such info-net firms will dominate the future.

Still, if there is unmanaged information in the value chain, it causes *negative* info-intensity and hurts market performance. But well-managed information creates *positive* info-intensity.

So glocal firms invest in info-movement and management (IM&M) systems. This boosts the velocity of their "info capital" *and* their market performance. Indeed, info-intensity can:

- Redefine products and entire industries;
- Spawn new or advanced products; and
- Boost product value.

• Redefine products and entire industries

Real estate firms such as **Century 21** don't sell homes; they broker computerized multiple listing information *about* homes. They help you decide what and where to buy, how much to pay, and how to finance the purchase. Similarly, banks with automated teller networks found they were not in the money business but in the business of information *about* money.

Banc One thus has spent $100 million reengineering its transaction processing system. Says President Donald McWhorter:

We're in the information business, not the transaction business. We want a system that gives us everything there is to know about the customer — and that "incidentally" handles the transaction.

Reuters, the world's leading information utility, aims to be not just an information source but a "dealing arena." As one of many services, the company collects and sells information on foreign currencies, money market trading, stocks and bonds, oil and commodities, and shipping. Rather than merely selling this knowledge, it aims to electronically link buyers and sellers worldwide, replacing local exchanges.

Info-networks thus reconstitute the marketplace and reconfigure the customer value chain into a value web. In this way, **American Airlines'** *Sabre* system became an essential "core" of the air transport web. Such innovations always change the competitive environment in favor of those introducing them.

• Spawn new or advanced products

In a glocal market, a product can have a short life cycle or quickly become an uncompetitively priced commodity. And there often is no time for global product rollouts because of "me-too" products springing up in local markets. To overcome these problems, glocal companies will start using virtual reality to "test market" products and then roll them out globally.

Even then, firms still need to develop tailored products in short order. Only a cross-functional team, linked by an info-network, can do this. Consider just these two examples.

Otis (part of **United Technologies**) put together a glocal elevator development team. French workers made the door systems, small-geared parts were made in Spain, the electronics in Germany, and special motor drives in Japan. The U.S. division did the systems integration, cutting development time 50% and creating an advanced elevator.

Boeing has promised **United Parcel Service** that it will custom-design and build 30 all-cargo versions of the *767* jet in a mere 33 months versus the usual 42 months. All 400 people working on the new freighter are grouped into teams which combine skills in design, planning, manufacturing, and tooling. Using a tele-computer network to coordinate activity and avoid rework, the project is ahead of schedule and budget.

• Boost product value

When new or extra information is bundled *into* a product, consumers often place higher value on it. Such info might make the product easier to use or better describe its benefits. For example, to promote CD players, **Sony** ran detailed ads in *Stereo Review* and *High Fidelity* magazines to reach musical elites. The ads took pains to "educate" — to explain how and why the CD players were a breakthrough in audio sound reproduction. Audiophiles and dealers raved about the players, and people flocked to the stores to buy.

Lederle Labs, the pharmaceutical arm of **American Cyanamid**, also raises the info-intensity of products to educate users about their value. The company developed a special education package on middle ear infection, the third most common childhood illness in America. The package consists of a videotape for parents to view in the doctor's office and a storybook for children to take home. Says group VP, Dave Bethune:

Service is built into our core values. From RD&E through manufacture, marketing, distribution, to the point of use, our prime consideration is meeting customer needs.

Entrepreneurial Accountability

Local decisions also help firms boost market share, profit, and stock market value. To gain most from glocal info-intensity, brands must become more like entrepreneurial units.

The Japanese are strong believers in local autonomy and in tailoring marketing to local conditions. **Nissan**, for example, is global in "upstream" marketing (strategy) but highly localized in "downstream" functions (advertising). Market execution is left entirely to local managers. Eisake Toyama, president of **Nissan Canada**, observes:

I don't think anybody back in Tokyo headquarters can really tell what Canadian customers want.

"Glocalization" implies optimally located decisions — on RD&E, production, advertising, packaging, sales, and service. To forge sustaining relationships with local customers, **Campbell Soup** divided its American salesforce into 21 independent regions, each in charge of local market planning and spending. This strategy, duplicated globally, is explained by Herbert Baum, **Campbell**'s president for north-south America, as follows:

We strategize and resource globally, manufacture regionally, and market locally. Viewing local markets from a global perspective, we leverage brand strengths while keeping a tight focus on local customer preferences.

While global scope is built on local scale penetration, in turn, a firm's increasing global market strength gives it a big edge in local markets. Other good examples of this strategy are franchise chains and multilevel marketers. They leverage their global brand image, global sourcing, and financial strength to optimize local market success.

To assess local financial performance, **Economic Value Added (EVA)** is becoming the primary measure of business units and of true return on investment (ROI). EVA accounts for the *total* cost of capital to measure *real* aftertax profit *(see box, overleaf)*.

Too many firms pursue short-term profits over customer satisfaction. They focus on the stock market and not enough on the real market. Yet, as Lew Platt, CEO of **Hewlett-Packard** observes:

Stock price is an outcome of the actions you take, not a driver of them.

How well a company uses its shareholder equity determines market value. Yet the cost of that equity doesn't appear in financial statements because most companies regard it as free! Roberto Goizueta, CEO of **Coca-Cola** explains EVA simply:

We raise capital to make concentrate, sell it at an operating profit, and pay the cost of capital. Shareholders pocket the difference.

Obviously, you can boost EVA in three ways:
- **Earn more with the same capital**. While OK, simple cost cuts can blind you to other sources of EVA.
- **Use less capital to raise effectiveness**. Thus, **Coca-Cola** switched from costly metal containers to plastic ones, **CSX** used 100 locomotives as efficiently as 150, and **Quaker Oats** rejigged production to cut warehouse costs.
- **Invest only in high-return projects** (i.e., those that yield *more* than their *total* cost of capital).

The EVA bottom line is clear: If your firm's EVA is positive, you created wealth; if negative, you destroyed capital!

CALCULATING EVA

Operating Profit *less* Taxes	= (A) After-tax profit
Total Capital *times* Weighted average cost of capital	= (B) Total cost of capital
(A) *minus* (B)	= Economic Value Added

Weighted average cost of capital has two components:
- interest cost of borrowed capital (say 7%);
- cost of equity (that is, "opportunity cost" of what shareholders would earn in price appreciation and dividends on a portfolio of other companies of similar risk). Over time, shareholders earn 6% more on stocks than on long-term bonds. So, if bonds earn 5%, the true cost of equity is 11%.

If a firm has 40% debt and 60% equity, its weighted average cost of total capital is:

40%	60%	
7%	11%	
2.80% +	6.60%	= 9.40%

Total capital includes real estate, machines, vehicles, etc., *plus* investments in RD&E and training (whether or not you treat them as operating expenses) *plus* working capital. If aftertax operating profit is $1 billion and total capital is $10 billion, the cost of capital is $940 million, creating an EVA of $60 million.

"Glocal" Costing and Pricing

Another new accounting method also improves entrepreneurial responsibility by glocalizing costs and prices.

Activity-Based Costing (ABC) tags costs at each step of the value chain, pinpointing efficiencies. While ordinary costing overlooks bottlenecks or downtime, ABC nails down all overheads, tagging them to products that use them, to highlight true efficiency.

The premise is that overhead/direct costs stem from activities that consume resources such as salaries, benefits, and rent. The goal is to identify activity costs and allocate them either to a product, vendor, or customer to determine their profitability. For example, invoice matching involves two activities: checking for a match and resolving any nonmatch. These activities should be costed separately and allocated to each vendor, not to the total cost of sales.

ABC thus tags direct/indirect activity cost to identify activities that add no value to the customer. It also measures profitability at the individual category, vendor, or item level. ABC thus focuses on the efficiency of the value chain.

The goal is to relentlessly strip time and costs from the supply chain through paperless "info-flow" systems. Each and every activity must be questioned. If it does not add value, ways must be found either to eliminate the activity or make it less costly. **At Boeing**, for example, Ronald Woodard, head of the commercial plane group, says:

We are convinced that 35%-40% of everything we do is nonvalue added. We intend to cut unit costs 25% by 1998 and speed delivery time for smaller planes from 12 months to just 6 months.

ABC also helps firms focus on glocal comparative advantage, which can't be measured against industry standards. Success stems from doing better in your economy *relative* to how a competitor performs in its economy. A *global* firm becomes a *glocal* cost leader by being more efficient in *local* markets.

By identifying what creates glocal value, ABC also links cross-functional teams and helps product designers reduce price (i.e., boost customer value) from the outset. This shifts the firm's focus to return on sales (ROS) — the true measure of success in the glocal market.

Japanese firms are obsessed with sales rather than profit. As noted, low inflation means that global price competition will intensify during the upswing of the new economic long-wave. However, inflation will vary between markets. Hence, firms must push profit responsibility down to local levels. Japanese pricing reverses our practice. We specify the product and tot up its component costs, adding overheads and profit to get price. Japanese firms start with desired market share, estimating what price will make that share feasible. Then they push down all costs until the market-based price is achieved.

This is not product "dumping." It is a core competency of glocal marketing! It drives down costs and boosts value added.

4. Community Ethics *(Ethical Capital)*

The fourth core competency is ethical capital built through the virtue of sustainable development. Sustainable economics involve meeting the needs of the present without compromising the ability of future generations to meet their needs. America used to be the model of the so-called "virtuous cycle" of democratic state capitalism. Today's buyers demand a return to ethical corporate behavior which is both:
   • "Glocal" Community-Based; and
   • Environmentally sound.

"Glocal" Community Ethics
By definition, glocal marketing is rooted in local *and* global community needs. Market presence must benefit a consumer's glocal community, the *Global Village*. And, to be socially responsible, a company should be "glocalized" in all aspects related to customer values.

Indeed, a truly glocal firm is so much a part of the *Global Village* that it is "stateless." It has *no* national identity; it is borderless, cosmopolitan, and multicultural. It is loyal to the glocal citizenry. Wherever a firm calls "home," info-networks make it a stateless firm, and its employees are glocal citizens. An E-mail address is their global passport.

NEC, the Japanese electronics giant, thus practices "Holonic Management" which it describes as the harmony of opposites. Matching the *Global Village* metaphor, **NEC** unites *holos* (the whole) and *on* (the individual) into a *holonic* or glocal synergy of people, technology, money, information, and culture. Kiyofumi Sakaguchi, president of **Prudential Japan**, says his role is to direct the process of "global localization," transferring the company's global value system to the local Japanese marketplace through a "delicate fusion process."

Similarly, **Nomura Securities** offers its clients: *"A global response to individual needs."* **Nomura** recognizes that *"global and local trends interact faster than* *ever; boundaries shift, market borders fade."* It views customer investment needs in an overall context and, no matter how modest the scale, *"fine-tunes each from a global perspective."*

To stateless companies, boundaries are only a state of mind. That's why **Coca-Cola** banned the words *domestic* and *foreign* from internal use. It no longer views the market from a U.S. perspective. Indeed, **Coke**'s business in America is secondary. In 1991, it earned 80% of its profit outside the U.S. market. By the year 2000, the U.S. market will account for no more than 10% of profit. As noted, to build a better sense of the glocal market, **Coke** has a new *"Multi-Local"* strategy. The firm's Cuban-born CEO, Roberto Goizueta, says it won't succeed without the theme, which he describes as:

A *binding mechanism that holds the company, the system, the brands, the consumer together.*

Stateless firms also have glocal vision and ethical values. They recognize that the *Global Village* is an amorphous mix of laws, morals, standards, and behavior. But, guided by conscience, their "spirit of enterprise" fosters employee self-esteem and proud teamwork in providing the market with ethical products.

Environmentally Sound Products/Services
Ecology is a key marketing frontier, and Japanese firms were first to see the market benefits. They led the "green" drive through what they call *kokoro* ecology:

The unity of mind, heart, and spirit that can save the planet through empathy and feeling for living beings.

Toyota's "green" program *(see box, below)* is based on the concept of *kyosei*. This two-part word means "together" *(kyo)* and "to live" *(sei)*, or "coexistence: living/working together for the common good."

Canon also adopted *kyosei* toward its clients, dealers, partners, and local communities. Company chairman Ryuzaburo Kaku says:

"Kyosei" stresses fair competition and mutual benefit plus a strong commitment to community and the environment.

TOYOTA'S ENVIRONMENTAL PROGRAM

Based on the *kyosei* philosophy of existing and prospering alongside local communities, Toyota developed an environmental and social-responsibility approach with three main precepts:
• Promote environmental measures that foster trust by the local community;

- Always set farsighted targets and environmental measures;
- Promote environmental measures for the industry as a whole.

To that end, the company's goals for new vehicles are:
- Ensure service centers recover/recharge equipment without any escape of CFCs;
- Use only air conditioners with HFC-134a refrigerant after 1994.

To cut factory and auto emissions such as SO_2, Toyota began promoting low-sulphur fuel in 1971 and cut the average sulphur content of heavy oil from 2.4% to 0.5% by 1978. To counter nitrogen oxide (NO_x) pollution, it improved the combustion of boilers at its plants, and a stringent energy-conservation program cut CO_2 emissions.

The firm also developed water-based car paints to cut volatile organic compounds (VOCs) and adopted high-efficiency techniques to minimize waste paint. Since 1975 the firm has slashed the volume of water used in vehicle production by 72% and now recycles at least 98% of all water used. It even treats rainwater that falls onto company property as contaminated. All wastewater released into rivers is cleaner than that of either the rivers themselves or local public-sewer processing facilities.

Hitachi also began going "green" in the 1970s and has won several awards. It quit using CFCs as a cleaning agent in making microchips and replaced CFCs and trichlorethanes in products. President Tsutomu Kanai says:

We have a global responsibility to be a good citizen. Every aspect has to be environmentally conscious.

Similarly, **Fuji Bank** shows a keen sensitivity to a greener quality of life. Its glocal environmental marketing slogan is:

Banking Ecology: Meeting client needs is half the story; meeting society's needs is the other half.

Genuine ecological concern takes market-driven firms beyond waste management and pollution cleanup. They stress *prevention* at the outset. Instead of using "end-of-pipe" technology (which incurs an add-on expense), they focus on "front-of-pipe" technology. Although this needs up-front investment, it raises process efficiency and is thus inherently thrifty *(see box of chemical industry examples, page 88)*.

Proactive environmental thinking also leads to high-value and high-virtue products. Market-focused companies build ecological soundness into the entire value chain, using a lifecycle or "cradle-to-grave" analysis of the product. Starting with product design, this covers manufacture, packaging, distribution, use by the consumer, and final recycling or disposal.

Xerox's *Environmental Leadership Program (ELP)* uses this approach to product design, and the firm has eliminated the use of ozone-depleting materials in its products and processes. Environmental concerns even take priority over economic considerations, and the company is committed to designing recyclable and reusable products. Among other things, the company has reclaimed millions of pounds of metals from used photoreceptors each year since 1965.

In 1993, the firm also activated America's largest fleet of low-emission, methanol-powered autos — using **GM**'s *Chevrolet Lumina.* In 1994, it also got a fleet of flex-fuel **Ford** *Taurus* sedans, running on an unleaded gas-methanol mix. For these and other actions, the World Environmental Center awarded **Xerox** its 1993 *Gold Medal for International Corporate Environmental Achievement.*

AT&T, also adopting life-cycle analysis, uses *Design for Environment* software to choose the least harmful materials, reduce energy use, cut hazardous waste, and make products easier to recycle. The final goal is "closed loop" business activity that emits no discharges and recycles everything.

In the food sector, polystyrene fast-food cartons were a vivid symbol of a throwaway society. But that changed fast in 1990 when **McDonald's** joined with Environmental Defense Fund to "reduce, reuse, and recycle." It now uses less packaging, uses less chlorine-bleached paper, and switched to smaller napkins. It ships ketchup and other garnishes in reusable crates and recycles or composts paper, food scraps, and cartons. The chain also uses recycled materials to outfit new stores.

Heinz, the food giant, cut its use of energy to help clean the environment. The firm uses a cogeneration plant to supply its main Canadian food processing facility with power. The plant converts natural gas to electricity and steam, recovers 80% of the exhaust for further use, and sells surplus electricity to the local utility which can reduce its generating capacity.

The U.S. auto industry takes its lead from California's tough environmental standards which require that 2% of car sales in the state be "zero emission" by 1998, rising to at least 10% of sales by 2003. Several other states have passed similar laws. **GM**, for one, has responded with a commitment to build an advanced electric sports car, the *Impact*, which it plans to market soon. Other car firms are following suit and have joined the Advanced Battery Consortium to make electric vehicle batteries. *(See box on page 89 for other U.S. auto examples.)*

North American gasoline retailers are also switching to "ecological correctness." **Mohawk Oil**, with 300 gas stations in western Canada, serves only ethanol-enriched gasoline which cuts carbon monoxide and other emissions by 40%. With a slogan of *"We struck wheat!"* and dubbing itself *Mother Nature's*

"Green" Chemical Industry

• **3M**'s *Pollution Prevention Pays* program is world-famous for its cost savings ($1 billion since 1975) and favorable environmental impact. By 1995, the firm will have cut air and water emissions by 90% and solid waste by 50% from 1990 levels. This investment will *reduce* overall costs by 10%. In 1991, the company's *Scotch-Brite* plant in Canada replaced the solvent-based resins used to bind the product's abrasives. Solvent emissions were cut by 65%, lower costs boosted productivity by 45%, and customers got a better product.

• **Dow**'s *Waste Reduction Always Pays (WRAP)* program cut air emissions 50% between 1985 and 1991, *saving* $10 million per year. A new ethylene plant in Alberta uses 40% less energy and releases 97% less wastewater. The higher cost is more than offset by less upkeep.

• **Hoechst Celanese** spent $500 million to cut pollution by 70%. The final goal of its *Waste & Release Reduction (WARR)* campaign is zero emissions. The firm joined with **Coca-Cola** to develop the first-ever plastic soft-drink bottle made with a blend of recycled plastic.

• **American Cyanamid**, aiming to exceed its 50% pollution reduction goal by 1995, is spending $50 million to reduce toxic releases by 80% by recovering 120 million pounds per year of chemicals such as sulfuric acid. The firm also worked with **John Deere**, the farm equipment maker, to develop a safe handling system for crop insecticide. The product, named *Lock 'n Load*, comes in a returnable and refillable plastic container. The container's special valve "docks" with a compatible valve on **Deere** planter boxes. This stops leakage during loading/removal, and there's no packaging to dispose of. **American Cyanamid**'s president Al Costello takes personal responsibility for environmental matters:

If there's a way to fix it, we'll fix it. We want to be recognized as responsible and concerned about places where we operate. I aim to work myself out of this environmental job!

• **DuPont** has a similar philosophy, as CEO Edgar Woolard asserts:

We must become aware of ourselves as environmentalists. As CEO, I am DuPont's chief environmentalist.

Gas Station, the company plans to install battery chargers at all its service stations to top up electric cars. Such charging stations are already appearing in Los Angeles, and the world's first electric car dealership opened in Hollywood in 1992.

"GREEN" MARKETING STRATEGIES
— U.S. Auto Industry —

• **America's "Green" Car Consortium**: In 1993, **GM**, **Ford**, and **Chrysler** joined a U.S. government-led public-private alliance to design "the car of the future" — a perfectly efficient, earth-friendly car for the 21st century. The aim is to produce a 80-miles-per-gallon (33-kilometers-per-liter), safe, low polluting, and affordable prototype within a decade. Initial research is on advanced catalysts to power lean-burn engines and electric power systems such as flywheels and ultracapacitors.

• **Chrysler** has won California approval for an electric version of its *Dodge Caravan* minivan. The 1993 model was certified by the Air Resources Board four years ahead of the 1998 deadline for zero emission vehicles. The van is powered by 30 six-volt nickel-iron (or nickel-cadmium) batteries which have a 100,000 mile life. It also has a regenerative braking system, which helps recharge the batteries when the brakes are applied. The van's top speed is 110 kilometers per hour, reaching 85 kilometers per hour in 27 seconds and running 133 kilometers between charges.

• **Ford** made 3,000 flexible-fuel *Taurus* cars, 200 natural gas-powered *Crown Victoria* sedans, and almost 100 *Ecostar* minivans in 1993. By 1996, it plans large-scale output of methanol/gas/electric vehicles. Flexible-fuel vehicles burn a liquid fuel that is 85% methanol plus gasoline, reducing harmful emissions by 30%. **Ford**'s *Synthesis 2010* all-aluminum family sedan weighs only 2,200 pounds, 46% less than a comparable steel-bodied car. Using special adhesives in place of welds, the car is 98% recyclable.

• **Hughes Aircraft** (part of **GM**) has created alternating-current (AC) motors that outperform the direct-current (DC) motors so far used in most electric vehicles. On an electric version of **GM**'s *Geo Prizm*, the DC motor boosted the car's range from 60 to 100 miles and dropped its acceleration time (to 50 miles per hour) from 30 to 13 seconds.

In general, a "green" consciousness pervades world business:

- More than 600 American firms belong to the EPA's *"33/50"* program to cut emissions 33% by 1992 and 50% by 1995.
- More than 500 firms signed the *Business Charter for Social Development* of the International Chamber of Commerce (ICC) which, by the way, was drafted by Edgar Woolard, CEO of **DuPont** *(see other reference at end of box on page 88).*
- The Business Council for Sustainable Development, a global body of 50 prominent CEOs, advocates the ICC principle of "compliance and reporting" *(see box, below).*

CORPORATE ENVIRONMENTAL REPORTING

Environmental reporting is a key element of competitive advantage and an effective tool to measure/communicate a firm's "green" commitment and progress. Annual *Environmental Reports* should cover:

• **Statement of Corporate Policy**
(policy, goals, priorities, steps taken, measurement);
• **Issues Relevant to the Firm**
(company-particular issues/initiatives and their impact);
• **Direct Resources Used**
(natural resources extraction, water use, etc., and their impact);
• **Energy Use**
(consumption by type of use);
• **Indirect Resources Used**
(materials, packaging, etc., and their impact);
• **Waste Generation and Management**
(landfill and reuse/recycle tonnages);
• **Toxic/Hazardous Products**
(cleaners, pesticides, solvents, treatment chemicals, CFCs, etc.);
• **Accidents and Risks**
(number/severity of spills, emissions, land remediation, etc.);
• **Pollutants**
(air/water/land, by type of pollutant);
• **Environmental Spending**
(capital costs, training expenses, community activity);
• **Legal Compliance**
(performance, audit results, discussion of legislation).

Through such efforts, *"high-value/high-virtue"* products are developed and sold. The *Impact*, for example, is a powerful yet ecologically friendly car. Its owners won't have to worry about having fun at the environment's expense. Such products have a distinctive competitive edge, building customer loyalty and brand equity.

Checklist for "Glocal" Marketers

Glocal firms need to respond to market forces and changed customer expectations with four sets of "core" competencies:

Employee Empowerment
- ✓ Develop "human capital" by nurturing people's natural curiosity to learn.
- ✓ Put your *"Learning Resource Center"* on-site, and provide menu-driven, self-learning computer modules for all educational programs.
- ✓ Revamp education programs to help people develop glocal instincts and trans-cultural/gender skills and values.
- ✓ Empower people to create a boundaryless customer focus.
- ✓ Use a no-frontiers recruiting policy and move people through glocal career paths.
- ✓ Institute an *"Honored Guest"* program to make sure you always treat customers properly.

Proprietary Products
- ✓ Invest in RD&E innovation, in critical technologies or key fields of expertise, to become a core techno-leader.
- ✓ Form a *"Technology Council"* and use glocal product mandating, concurrent engineering, real-time telecom RD&E networks, and BIMMS.
- ✓ "Electrify" all processes.
- ✓ "Informationalize" all products.
- ✓ Institute an *"Efficient Customer Response"* (ECR) system.

Information Intensity
- ✓ Shift value-chain activity closer to the customer through info-movement and management (IM&M) networks.
- ✓ Create proprietary info-intensive "know banks."
- ✓ "Educate" buyers about your products and services.
- ✓ Delegate full responsibility to locally accountable entrepreneurial marketers for all aspects of marketing and customer relations.
- ✓ Use *Activity Based Costing* (ABC) to "glocalize" prices and *Economic Value Added* (EVA) to measure true ROI and ROS.

Ecology Ethics

- ✓ Be driven by conscience and adopt a stateless *kyosei* mindset to become an ethical glocal corporate citizen.
- ✓ CEOs should take personal responsibility for environmental matters because CEO also means "Chief *Environmental* Officer."
- ✓ Join the EPA's *"33/50"* program and subscribe to the International Chamber of Commerce's *Business Charter for Social Development*.
- ✓ Help restore the environment with a sound value chain, offering only "green" products to gain a distinct, glocal competitive edge.
- ✓ Publish an annual *Environmental Report* for your company.

Together, these "core" competencies are essential if your firm is to develop a glocal marketing culture, discussed in Step Four.

CREATE AN
INFO-NETWORK CULTURE

*Culture is the difference between short-term goals and
long-term vision. Marketing means getting each customer
to love your company, your products, and your service.*

—Hank Johnson, retired CEO, **Spiegel**

To capitalize on their core competencies, leading firms are busy "re-engineering" themselves to achieve full synergy with the *Global Village* market through a glocal marketing info-network culture.

This culture will be based on four inspiring values which mirrors the rest of the Glocal Marketing Model:

1. Passionate Caring
2. Powerful Communication
3. Cooperating to Compete
4. Societal Commitment

1. Passionate Caring (not *Couldn't Care Less*)

Caring companies are always eager to learn what customers want — and then provide it. They motivate employees to *care passionately* about customers by:
- Creating an Info-Network Structure;
- Forming Self-Directed Workteams;
- Trusting People;
- Empowering People to Care;
- Doing the Unexpected; and
- Getting Close to the Local Customer.

Creating an Info-Network Structure
People who work in pyramids care only about escaping them. Pyramids are tombs for dead pharaohs. Pyramids don't move; they just slowly crumble. Hence, simply to remove layers from a pyramid merely yields a more claustrophobic tomb.

Fortunately, the Info Revolution shatters corporate pyramids. You see, the "hierarchy" of information (if it even has one) is as flat as that of the printed circuit boards which process it. Information naturally organizes itself into patterns and is easily managed by computerized telecom networks. Such networks are the "info-structures" around which all societies and markets are inevitably being reorganized. Only firms with a parallel info-network structure will be agile enough to use the power of new telecom technologies to gain a glocal edge.

Using hierarchy and bureaucracy, the "Organizational Man" of the 1950s turned companies into stifling pyramids. In the 1970s, horizontal and vertical integration made companies unwieldy. To try to overcome this, strategic business units (SBUs) were created, leading to the 1980s' idea of market segmentation. But mega-firms then blindly tried to segment globally.

These monoliths lack the agility needed to cope with *Global Village* fluidity. Rigidly hierarchic, their value chains are ramrod linear and too focused on production-line quality. Their often arrogant marketing efforts are purely product-driven.

As **IBM, GM**, and other aged monsters found, society is an info-network and marketing is consumer-driven. Old structures — whether pyramid or hybrid matrix, whether organized around functions, geography, divisions, or product lines — are obsolete. All will be replaced by customer-focused teams grouped in an info-network design. Rather than being stifled by bureaucracy, their scope and scale will be enhanced by their info-network's local vibrancy.

Any executive knows that the traditional organization chart long-ago became inadequate. They see significant systemic principles in the world around them. They know intuitively that corporate communications channels stretch through space and time, taking on a new shape as the "info-structure" evolves, much like cells dividing and redividing.

More than a dozen years ago in *Planning Review* (November 1981), I proposed an organic representation of how companies would operate in the Info Age. Today, it is even more clear that hierarchic structures must be replaced by a membranelike pattern which resembles a cellphone system. I propose the "cellular honeycomb" design *(depicted overleaf)*.

With this simple redesign, a company's key processes, core competencies, and customer linkages become clear. Functional isolation is eliminated, and it is apparent that the company functions as an organic whole which "mirrors" its customer base.

Centrally, the CEO is supported by "manager owners" of core competencies, process flows, or customer types. In large firms, a "Coordination Center" manages customer-driven teams organized around customer-relevant core competencies or process flows. Departmental reporting channels and job descriptions are replaced by info-flows and job skills.

"CELLULAR HONEYCOMB" ORGANIZATION DESIGN

Customer-Focused Teams
Organized Around Customer-Relevant
"Core" Competencies or Process "Flows"

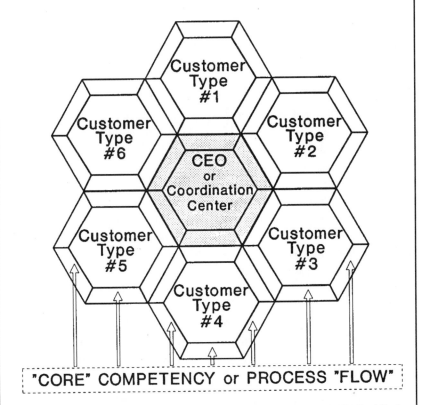

"CORE" COMPETENCY or PROCESS "FLOW"

The old hierarchic pyramid and new "cellular honeycomb" info-structure are quite different *(see table, opposite, which also provides examples of companies changing their culture)*.

Clearly, simply altering the structure is not enough. Neither is downsizing, which simply makes remaining jobs bigger and more difficult. It does nothing to improve how corporate work gets done; indeed, it can diminish efficiency. It is better to replace *all* "jobs" with a "portfolio of assignments" designed around the flow of key processes, essential core competencies, or customer types.

For these companies, customer satisfaction is the primary measure of performance, with rewards based on skills or competencies, not output, profits, or job tasks. And, since the glocal challenge is beyond individual performance, corporate culture must become team-driven and market-focused.

Forming Self-Directed Workteams

The best way to generate individual enthusiasm is to group people in self-directed workteams focused on customer types, key processes, or competencies. Let's review some examples.

Xerox has changed its structure, work processes, and job assignments — and how it empowers people — to regroup around types of customers. Closest to the customer is the operational level, made up of nine business teams and local sales and service people. These entrepreneurial units serve markets such as small businesses, individuals, and office documents and engineering systems. The teams take new technology from research, develop it into products (with customer input), and then make them. They also do product planning and marketing, delivering a complete package to the salesforce.

At **Xerox**, customer relations are coordinated by a one-stop *Customer Operations Group* which links sales, shipping, installation, service, and billing. This group "buys" internally from "focussed factories" dedicated to specific local markets.

SHIFT TO "CELLULAR" ORGANIZATION DESIGN		
Vertical Pyramid Box Structure	**Info-Network Cell Structure**	**Company Examples**
Rigid structure built around functions or geography.	Cluster around core processes or competencies or customer types.	**Chrysler**'s process approach to develop *Neon* sub-compact at a fraction of typical cost.
Put people in departments.	Group people in self-managed teams accountable for measurable perform-ance goals.	**Kodak**'s *Eastman Chemical* ditched Snr VPs of R&D, production, and adminis-tration, setting up 1,000 self-directed teams.
Reward increases in profits or output.	Make customer satis-faction the primary driver and measure of team performance.	**AT&T**'s *Network Systems* awards bonuses based on customer evaluations.
Pay for individual job performance.	Reward team-based skills acquisition and application based on peer review.	**GE** uses "360° appraisal" by peers and those above and below the employee, basing pay on skills developed and teamwork.
Downsize, lay people off, expand jobs.	Combine fragmented tasks into skill portfolios and eliminate work that fails to add value.	**AT&T** units do annual budgets based on comprehensive processes such as full telecom network maintenance.

Hence, market forces extend back from the customer, through the entire "flow." Describing these "micro-enterprise units," **Xerox** CEO Paul Allaire says:

We've turned a functional structure on its side and given teams end-to-end responsibility to bring products to the customer. All have a direct line of sight to the customer.

W. R. Grace is boosting its global telecom system by adding video and audio conferencing to its worldwide E-mail system. The goal is to help product-line managers respond quickly to customer needs and stay on top of competition. To increase its customer focus, **Grace** has eight manager-owners of core products, each with the title of president, in charge of developing core businesses. Says P. D. Bolduc, **Grace**'s CEO:

> I want customers to know that, wherever they buy, our products will be of consistent high quality and delivered on time. If customers are unhappy or want some changes they can directly reach one highly visible executive who will respond personally.

Northern Telecom also smashed its hierarchy, shifting power from central managers to self-directed local teams with diverse abilities. Factories were reorganized into team-based groups, collapsing functional departments into small process-driven units. These teams, which set their own shifts and chart their own productivity, are also paid salaries rather than wages. Within a year, quality improved by 50% and profits doubled.

Kodak groups employees into what it calls "the flow," not departments. Within this flow are "streams" of customer types. In these streams, people work in self-directed entrepreneurial teams which are scored on customer satisfaction measures. **Polaroid** divides its customers into three imaging groups (Family, Business, and Technical Industrial) and serves them through a team-based *Polaroid Express* telephone "Call Center" *(discussed in Part Five)*.

Binney & Smith (B&S), a crayon-making unit of **Hallmark Cards**, uses "high-velocity" teams. It scrapped hierarchy in 1991 and formed teams of cross-competent, multi-skilled workers. Team leaders report directly to the plant manager, and team members learn each other's jobs. Everyone can mold, label, collate, pack crayons, and run all machines. Each team is a mini-factory which manages scheduling, inventory, costs, machine upkeep, quality control, waste recycling, and customer service. Within a year, quality reached 100%, costs fell 32%, inventory fell 75%, output doubled, and profit climbed 140%.

Boeing's *777*, due out in 1995, is its first plane designed and built by teams of experts in design, manufacturing, and tooling. Customers are also involved in the design process. The same approach will be used for the *737X*, a passenger jet due out in 1997. The firm also uses 360° performance revues in which managers are evaluated by subordinates and peers as well as supervisors.

John Deere has grouped workers into self-directed teams at its factories. In one case, an overhaul of assembly line methods brought together 12 steps that had been scattered throughout the factory, cutting assembly costs by more than 10%. At another site, a just-in-time system speeded up deliveries from twice a month to twice a week, slashing inventory by about 20%. A third factory's cost-reduction suggestion system enabled the firm to cut design times by 33% between 1990 and 1993.

Phillips Cables (part of the **BICC** group) adopted self-directed workteams at its Brockville plant. It replaced 81 job classifications to 4 skills sets and grouped people into 20 cellular workteams or mini-factories.

Saturn (part of **GM**) has only two job classes, and workers get salaries not wages. Self-directed teams design their own work environment *(see box, below)*, with people rotating to learn the skills needed to get the job done. Company decision-making is fully participatory (on a *Member-to-Member* basis), taking all issues out to the whole company to gather input. Observes **Saturn** president Richard "Skip" LeFauve:

We teach people all about the business. Then they can input their perspective to our strategic business planning process. You simply get better business decisions and better business results.

SELF-DIRECTED WORKTEAMS AT SATURN CORPORATION

Saturn's self-directed work units accomplish tasks within their areas of responsibility without direction. Using a "shifting leadership" principle, work-unit members are empowered to make operational and planning decisions for their team in three main areas:

Work Flow Planning and Management
• Plan and decide their own work flow and methods.
• Obtain their own supplies and resources.
• Control their own material, inventory, and scrap.
• Perform their own equipment maintenance and repairs.
• Perform their own housekeeping.

Human Resource Planning and Management
• Select members into the work unit.
• Design their own jobs and make job assignments.
• Schedule vacations and arrange absentee replacements.
• Maintain/perform their own health and safety program.
• Help to develop and deliver training programs.
• Schedule communications within/outside the team.
• Schedule and hold their own meetings.
• Resolve their own conflicts.

Accountability and Responsibility
- Produce quality, cost-competitive products on time.
- Constantly improve quality/cost and work environment.
- Initiate consultation for self-corrective action.
- Keep their own records.
- Perform to their own budget.

(Source: Adapted from Saturn Corporation published documents)

Trusting People

Employee commitment cannot be "bought." Neither can it be directed or controlled. It can only be "earned" over time by consistent and enlightened management which treats people as important team members and trusts them.

Japanese firms are paternalistic, but they trust people. They know that the motivated commitment of the many is stronger than that of the few. They share information across the firm to provide context to employees, earning their respect and eager participation. Masao Kanei, chairman of **Sumitomo** explains:

It is the workers who actually make improvements and innovations. No increase in productivity can be expected unless management treats workers with greatest respect.

Trusting companies create a virtuous circle of caring. While they care about their employees, this does *not* mean that such companies put employees first and customers second. Firms that put customers second rarely finish first. Being client-driven, leading firms care about customers *through* caring employees. They remove every hurdle to smooth dealings with the customer. Thus empowered, people create an enthusiastic spirit of enterprise that always exceeds customer expectations.

Consider **Anixter**, an electrical wire and cable distributor with 140 locations worldwide. The company's philosophy is based on 10 values. The top three are:
- *People come first;*
- *Our word is our bond — we are reliable;*
- *We are serious about service.*

Its only policy manual is a 24-page pocket-sized *"Little Blue Book"* of only 1,100 words (I counted). Here are some gems:
- *Enthusiasm is the greatest business asset in the world.*
- *Customers don't depend on us; we depend on them.*
- *Lacking proprietary products, our service must be outstanding.*
- *To give sensational service, our people must really care.*

Empowering People to Care

To fully develop passionate caring, you must empower people with all the information, resources, and support they need to satisfy customers.

Rosenbluth Travel, America's largest corporate travel agency, is a prime example. Growing an amazing 8,000% (that is *not* a typo!) between 1975 and 1993, sales now approach $2 billion a year. The secret of this fabulous success is a unique blend of people, culture, technology, knowledge, custom-tailored products, and glocal market expansion. Above all, the company puts people first. Says chairman Hal Rosenbluth:

We care for, value, empower, and motivate people to care for their clients. This inspires a level of service that comes from the heart. It can't be faked.

When **Rosenbluth** hires people, "kindness, caring, compassion, and unselfishness" are more important than years of experience, salary history, or educational qualifications. The firm simply aims to have more "nice people" than its competitors. People are selected for what they "bring to the team" as much as for their personal potential. Especially important is their "fit" with the company's culture. Indeed, in nurturing a team culture, the firm does not use the word "employee" because it infers hireling, servant, or subordinate. Instead, staff are called associates, suggesting colleague, partner, or friend.

Rosenbluth has also invested heavily in info-systems. First, rather than depending on airline reservation systems, it became technically independent by creating its own *Readout* system. This proprietary software fuses airfare data from *all* major airlines into a single in-house system. Second, the company captures data on client travel patterns and uses it to negotiate airline discounts for clients. The in-house system thus gives the firm a big competitive edge and lets associates pool their expertise to serve clients better.

A related system, *Precision*, lets agents custom-tailor travel services to the personal needs of a client's employee. The system knows which employees may fly business or first class. Frequent flyer numbers are automatically entered, favorite seating reserved, and any special meal ordered. Hotel and car rental options are also preselected based on corporate travel policies. A third system, *Vision*, is a data base of all travel activity. Clients use electronic data interchange (EDI) to download their data from the system, meshing it with payroll and expense reporting systems. The system also provides a credit card reconciliation service.

The company's value package doesn't end there. It also takes time to educate clients about the company, its services, and the corporate travel business in general — all as a free, unexpected "purchase perk."

Doing the Unexpected

The **Four Seasons Hotel** group is famous for doing the unexpected. Even competitors view it as the world's premier-service hotel chain. To pamper guests, the hotel employs four staff members (again called associates) for every three guest rooms — double the industry norm. The hotel also pays above-average salaries, plus bonuses based on each hotel's profit. While costs are obviously high, rooms are 95% occupied versus the industry's 70% average.

Any modern hotel uses computer reservation systems. But **Four Seasons'** satellite-accessible guest history goes beyond the basics. It even records whether a guest asked for a specific kind of soap or an extra pillow on a previous visit. Moreover, the hotel deliberately does not publicize some of these extra personal service perks so it can pleasantly surprise you.

Nowhere is good treatment more important than in healthcare. This is a business where, hopefully, customers do *not* keep coming back but rather tell others about the wonderful care they received. Yet most hospitals are impersonal, production-line sickness-treating factories. A notable exception, the **Mayo Clinic**, uses the motto: *The best interest of our patient is our only interest.*

Every doctor is on salary, so there is no incentive to boost income by seeing many patients. Indeed, there's no time limit on how long a doctor spends with a patient. Group practice is the norm, and patient care drives research and education, not *vice versa*. From routine physicals to complex surgery, a team of specialists jointly diagnose treatment. They constantly stress thorough investigation and clear explanation.

The central clinic (in Rochester, Minnesota) is the hub of other **Mayo** hospitals which are linked by satellite. This tele-medicine network is used to send x-rays, lab reports, and diagnoses across hundreds of miles in tele-consultations between doctors and technicians. While such "high-touch/high-tech" care is not cheap, **Mayo** also provides unexpected perks such as inexpensive lodging for patients' families and visitors.

Even fast-food chains can provide exceptional service. I once found my local **McDonald's** packed with softball players. While the lineup moved fast, it took some time for me to get my family's order. Indeed, the place was so busy I was served by the manager. Imagine my astonishment when he said my entire tab was "On the house!" He explained that I had waited 12 minutes (he was doing the timing, not me), and this was unacceptable to him. He apologized and hoped I'd come back.

Well, I've certainly returned. And I've told that story hundreds of times to audiences across North America. In short, one local manager's empowered initiative reaped abundant word of mouth for **McDonald's**.

Getting Close to the Local Customer

Again, "serving" the *local* customer rather than "selling" the *global* product is the key to *glocal* market success. Caring companies delegate power and engender glocal independence. As MIT's Peter Senge observes in *The Fifth Discipline*: *Learning companies always localize. They extend the maximum degree of authority and power as far from the top or corporate center as possible.*

Club Med, for example, runs its villages as independent units, each hiring its own staff and taking advantage of local conditions and amenities. The personal touch includes calling staff GOs (meaning *gentils organisateurs*, or "nice organizers") and guests GMs (*gentils membres*, or "nice people"). At each village, the staff is multiethnic, and they live on site to better serve their multicultural clientele.

Frito-Lay, the snack-food arm of **PepsiCo**, serves retailers with a localized salesforce. They deliver product and restock shelves based on each store's precise needs. At **Alpac**, a **Pepsi**bottler in Seattle, marketing managers decide their own ad programs, and delivery truck drivers decide how much volume they'll move in a day. Explains CEO Carl Behnke:

If a store asks for something, the driver can satisfy it without checking with a supervisor first.

Such "close-to-the-local-customer" involvement also boosts product innovation. In a customer-focused culture, everybody gets involved in local marketing.

Japanese firms send market-oriented product-design engineers into local markets for six months every year to talk with customers and study their needs. **Sony** developed the *Walkman* in 1979 after its touring engineers spotted California roller skaters toting portable radios. Since then, it has developed more than 260 different models. That's one every three weeks!

In 1991, **Sony** got closer still to North American consumers, opening its first *Gallery of Consumer Electronics* in Chicago. While also a retail outlet, the *Gallery* is staffed by market-oriented engineers and is a customer research lab. It exposes buyers to multimedia technology in nonthreatening lifestyle settings such as a home office.

Sony engineers thus gain "high-touch" contact with buyers, without any filtering by distributors, sales people, or market researchers. They care passionately about buyer satisfaction.

2. Powerful Communication (not *Command & Control*)

In a glocal marketing culture, as the previous examples show, info must flow to where it's needed, unfiltered by hierarchy and stifling bureaucracy. Customers are used to an instant response. They are no longer willing to wait days or even hours for service. Tomorrow is simply too late. Glocal marketers need:

• A Customer-Driven Info-Structure;

• Small Company Responsiveness; and
• "Virtual" Networks.

Customer-Driven Info-Structure

There are 10 steps to a customer-driven info-structure *(see box, below)*, most of which has been discussed already.

In such an info-network structure, top managers find they don't need to control. Indeed, they can better orchestrate the firm's marketing activity. Thanks to feedback loops, they can let go, empowering local managers and earning their commitment. In turn, this overcomes the need to control. Indeed, control is enhanced without controlling!

In after-sales service or customer support, info-networks place service personnel closer to the customer and gain instant customer feedback. A good example is **Polaroid**'s "Call Center" concept *(discussed on page 98 and again in Step Five).*

---

10 STEPS TO A CUSTOMER-DRIVEN INFO-STRUCTURE

• **Identify** strategic customer-driven objectives
• **Analyze** competitive advantages
• **Define** essential core processes/competencies
• **Organize** around customer-linked processes
• **Eliminate** all actions which don't add value
• **Appoint** "manager-owner" of each core process
• **Create** multi-skilled process teams
• **Set** customer-driven performance goals
• **Empower** employees with information
• **Adopt** skills/team-based training/rewards

Without info-networks, the following companies could not stand behind their well-known time-competitive slogans:

Bankers Trust:	*Served in seven minutes, or get a $5 bill.*
Deluxe Checks:	*48-hour turnaround, zero defects.*
Federal Express:	*Absolutely, positively, overnight.*

Time-based competition focuses on manufacturer-supplier links. While this can fall way short of the marketplace, the gap can be bridged with close links to the end consumer through the retailer. **Daiichi**, a Japanese electronics retailer, links time-based competition with buyers and employees via a powerful info-gathering system:

- The firm differentiates itself with a three-year rather than a one-year product warranty.
- A trained technician visits owners' homes to check products just before warranties expire.
- As a courtesy, the technician also checks other appliances in the home, regardless of brand or place of purchase.
- Data on the model/type/age of *all* products found in the home is then added to a data base.
- A follow-up letter to the customer confirms the health of the particular item bought from **Daiichi**.
- The customer is invited to come in to see new products which might be of interest.

As a result, 70% of sales are from repeat buyers, and the company's return on assets is five times the norm.

As well as speeding up deliveries and improving service, info-networks also reduce inventory. Indeed, as **FedEx** proves, inventories can no longer be treated as goods in storage. They are info-intensive items flowing through a network. Or, as Taichi Sakaiya, author of *The Knowledge Revolution*, observes:

The significance of material goods [will be] as containers or vehicles for knowledge-value.

Take **Union Pacific**, which constantly has 1,000 trains in transit. The trains are monitored through sensors connected to fiberoptic cables laid along the tracks. The rail network has become an info-network. As a result, instead of only 50% of deliveries arriving on time, 90% now do so. To solve the problem of "lost" railroad cars (sitting in sidings or rail yards), the company is putting bar codes on the cars. Trackside scanners, like those at supermarket checkouts, will identify passing cars. Observes chief information officer, Joyce Wrenn:

Large data bases lower our costs through better asset deployment and improve customer service. It's the only way to run a railroad.

Small Company Responsiveness

Market leaders use telecom networks so well that they have tiny headquarters. **Bata**, the world's [#]1 shoe company with a 40% market share, has 100 plants across global time zones. It coordinates them from a small two-story office in Toronto *via* a real-time info-network. Its culture is driven by the need to communicate intensely *without* controlling. The firm adopted a *"Multi-Domestic"* network design to gain "geographic flexibility." Explains chairman Thomas Bata:

Head office is a coordination center. We abandoned our regional-functional matrix because global priorities clash too often with local ones. Our inte-

grated network bridges the gap. And our new culture lets local units respond to the market within global priorities.

Similarly, **M&M Mars** runs the world's largest confectionery business with an info-network and a central management team of only 30 people. **Domino's Pizza** runs 5,000 stores in America with only 60 people at head office. **Monarch** is a soft-drink franchisor servicing 800 U.S. bottling plants and marketing its brands in 40 countries. It has a tiny Atlanta home office responsible only for administration and finance. After adopting its localized info-network, sales grew 500% in four years!

Telecom networks thus achieve small company responsiveness, placing value-chain action closer to the customer. Head office becomes a "customer switchboard," not a bureaucracy. Company boundaries are erased by the team-based culture.

"Virtual" Networks

Charles Savage, whose *Fifth Generation Management* is a teamworkers guidebook, envisions "virtual" teams. They share know-how and resources but constantly form and reform as the customer value chain requires. The "virtual corporation," the latest buzz phrase, denotes a completely different approach to business. In a flash, the virtual business creates what customers had only been thinking about just moments earlier. It changes our world as much as Henry Ford's assembly line did .

The Information Age makes tele-computer networks accessible to even the smallest enterprise: PCs, modems, and fax machines let you command on-line data bases, electronic banking, and E-mail on a glocal scale. The bottom line: The faster you get your service or product to market, the more profitable your business will be. Why? Because these flexible tools let you respond mid-stride to swings in consumer mood.

Xerox Canada, for instance, has unveiled a lab designed to bring products to market more quickly through computer modeling and simulation. The lab has networked workstations, an array of marketing and design software, and collaborative tools such as *LiveBoard*. Developed by **Xerox**, this interactive, multimedia tool allows workgroups in different locations to instantly collaborate through shared ideas and info. With a wireless pen, users draw directly on *LiveBoard*'s 5-foot-wide interactive surface. This creates an "electronic document" that is transferred via phone line to other sites for simultaneous viewing and participation.

Similarly, the sleek 1994 *Mustang* (named "Car of the Year" by *Motor Trend*) stems from the new way **Ford** designs cars. The company uses an integrated computer network to merge a collection of design studios scattered around the planet into a glocal design studio. Graphic workstations use mathematical models to transform sketches into lifelike, shiny cars that reflect their changing surroundings as they rotate on non-existent on-screen "turntables." Chief of international design, Jack Telnack calls the entire process *"virtual co-location"* of everyone involved in worldwide design.

Again, **AT&T** is using its *Safari* notebook computer to replace branch sales offices with "virtual" offices. The convergence of computers and telephones makes sales reps "location-independent" and lets them become entrepreneurial. Marketing experts can team together, "swarming" to serve one unique local customer after another.

Chiat/Day has reduced its office space by 40% to become the world's first virtual ad agency. Employees now use PCs and phones to work out of their homes or at clients' offices. Company chairman Jay Chiat likens traditional offices, with their regimented design, to *"kindergartens"* and calls them *"a 19th-century concept."* He's correct — on both scores!

In future, entire industries may become info-networked. A 1991 Lehigh University report, *21st-Century Manufacturing Enterprise Strategy*, draws heavily on Japan's glocal strategy. It envisions agile firms using a computer network linking every North American factory. Firms would use the info-network to form instant on-line partnerships, or what it calls "virtual ventures," to serve fast-moving markets. Products ordered electronically today could be built overnight, to precise customer specifications, and delivered next morning.

This is no idle dream. When computers are linked together in a high-speed network, they effectively "fuse" into a single entity, sharing each other's power. Such high-powered networks are "virtual laboratories" of fused information which moves at the speed of signals in the central nervous system.

In such a world, old patterns and old ways simply become irrelevant. Cooperation is essential to effective competition!

3. Cooperating to Compete (not *Blind Competition*)

Info-networks also make a cooperative culture superior to a competitive one. Win-win strategic alliances depend on:

- Information Sharing; and
- Strategic Alliances.

Information Sharing

Though internally developed know-how is vital, firms worry too much about intellectual property rights. This misplaced concern is a barrier to strategic alliances. Copyrights and patents monopolize knowledge and thus become self-defeating. Moreover, to claim ownership of "intellectual property" is futile in a real-time world where everyone can access a global "know-bank." Yoneji Masuda, the brain behind Japan's information society strategy, argues that the right of information *usage* will prevail over the right of *ownership*. He's right.

The free flow of ideas cannot be legislated; ideas are akin to fresh air and universal access is a birthright. Thus, Canada's Supreme Court says you can't "own" confidentiality; you can only "enjoy" it. Hence, nobody can "steal" know-how from you. Even the goal of intellectual property rights under the U.S. Constitution is *not* to reward knowledge creators but to further the public good. Indeed, knowledge *is* a public good. Hence, the surest way to avoid its "theft" — and to boost its value — is to share it.

This stems from the multiplier effect of shared information. If you protect info, keeping it secret, it loses value; when you share info, it gains value. And the faster and farther you move it, the more valuable it becomes. In sum, info-networks reverse the law of diminishing returns.

These mind-blowing anomalies of info-economics lead glocal firms to seek "network externalities." Like organic cells dividing and redividing, a network grows faster than the number of participants in it. And, as it grows, its value becomes so high that competitors must join or die.

For instance, **JVC** deliberately shared its *VHS* format for VCRs. This assured that most videocassettes used *VHS* format, pushing *Betamax* out of the market. **Sony** formed the *Compact Disc Group*, a coalition of disc and player makers, to establish a uniform CD format and assure **Sony**'s ability to compete.

Similarly, **DEC** joined the *Open Software Foundation* because its *VAX* operating system would be worth more if it were compatible with competing systems. **Citibank**, after trying to go it alone, joined the *Cirrus* automated teller network and promptly gained market share.

DEC also uses the **Internet**, as do other high-tech firms such as **GE, Hewlett-Packard, IBM, Intel**, and **Motorola**. Other big users are finance industry giants **J.P.Morgan** and **Charles Schwab** and automaker **Ford**.

Les Shoyer, VP/CIO of **Motorola** says info-networks are the most powerful business tool available. He observes:

Networks are our preferred way of exchanging scientific data and carrying out joint projects. We, our suppliers, and our customers place a high premium on rapid, robust info-flow.

Strategic Alliances

Such info-sharing is essential for successful strategic alliances. Info-networked firms can join local scale production units to optimize their global scope and glocal leverage.

As noted earlier, Japanese CEOs promote "coexistence with competitors at home and abroad" through *kyosei*, meaning "coexistence, or living/working together for the common good." In 1993, *kyosei* became the official slogan of KEIDANREN, Japan's most powerful business association.

Tadahiro Sekimoto, president of **NEC**, calls worldwide ventures *"mesh globalization"* and refers to strategic alliances as *"N&A"* (network and alliance). He says the role of *"N&A"* will broaden considerably in a borderless economy.

RD&E is simply becoming too expensive for most firms to go it alone. To overcome this barrier to innovation, expertise and costs must be pooled; synergies must be sought, strategic partnerships forged. RD&E alliances between firms, and with their local suppliers, will be a key factor of glocal market success for many companies, including large ones.

Indeed, to achieve glocal market success, outright mergers may be necessary. In the late 1990s, there will be a major consolidation of high-tech firms, especially in the computer and telecom sectors. The average cost of developing a new microchip or new software doubled in the 1980s and is doubling again in the 1990s. Companies thus need full marriage partners to share these costs and to access glocal markets to recoup them.

In tele-computers, some recent RD&E alliances are **Toshiba-IBM-Siemens, Hitachi-Texas Instruments, Fujitsu-AMD, Sharp-Intel, NEC-AT&T**, and **Matsushita-Intel**. These efforts ultimately will redefine the computer, telecom, and consumer electronics industries, fusing them together.

This strategy will work well under the North American Free Trade Agreement (NAFTA). Already, **Dominion Group** (Canada) uses an info-network to run an automobile wiring harness assembly plant in Juarez (Mexico) for **GM** (U.S.). It also supplies harnesses to **Honda** (Japan) in Ohio (U.S.) for **Sumitomo** (Japan). In this way, these info-intensive global manufacturers become synergistic assemblers in low-cost Mexico for local North American markets.

Such ventures are key to **Matsushita**'s glocal marketing strategy in NAFTA. In the multimedia field alone it has three alliances: *EO* (with **AT&T** and **Marubeni**); *3DO* (with **AT&T, Electronic Arts, MCA**, and **Time-Warner**); *General Magic* (with **AT&T, Apple, Motorola, Phillips**, and **Sony**). The firm also joined with **Whirlpool** in *Matsushita Floor Care* to make vacuum cleaners. This glocal venture links U.S. and Japanese management techniques and plugs into **Whirlpool**'s U.S. retail network. Most of the engineers are American and 98% of the components are bought locally.

Strategic alliances thus avoid local market rivalry. In the late 1980s, for instance, **Union Pacific** allied with a dozen regional truck lines, setting up a network that combined the economies of rail with the flexibility of trucks.

Cross-marketing alliances allow parallel product testing and simultaneous market roll-out. **Kao**, the Japanese household goods and toiletries company, worked with **Colgate-Palmolive** to introduce **Kao**'s products into the U.S. market. Instead of complaining about Japan's supposedly "closed" domestic market, **Colgate-Palmolive** drew on **Kao**'s info-network to launch its products there.

The success of alliances thus flows from a recognition of and respect for each partner's core competence, market interests, and operating independence. Using this maxim, **Corning Glass** has forged 40+ strategic alliances in a dozen countries, with only six failures over several decades. More than 50% of company profit now comes from ventures with the likes of **Siemens**, **Ciba Geigy**, **Samsung**, and **Asahi Glass**.

Info-networks also allow efficient subcontracting. **Kao** generates the same sales as a U.S. counterpart with only 12% of the payroll. It achieves this through strategic partnerships, using an info-network to link the best providers of services to a single market mission. The firm subcontracts everything from RD&E and production to the watering of plants in offices.

Another Japanese company, **Mitsubishi**, uses a *Mitsubishi International Data Network* to link its affiliates, buyers, and suppliers. Of course, not all global companies can afford their own telecom network. Moreover, 55% of the world has no phone service, presenting a big problem for global firms.

But this is a big opportunity for a satellite firm such as **COMSAT**. The company enters global markets along with its U.S. clients — large companies opening offices around the planet and needing info-network links. Joel Alper, president of **COMSAT Systems**, observes:

> *Our partners know the local environment. They offer us the flexibility to adapt to changing local conditions. Local managers know the language and the culture and can more easily find markets for our technology.*

Once it becomes locally established, **COMSAT** sells communications services to other global firms and to local companies needing to communicate with the world.

Paradoxically, then, through vigorous *local cooperation*, info-networked firms gain a unique *global competitive* advantage in the *glocal* market.

4. Societal Commitment (not *Empty Platitudes*)

Global competition is no longer firm to firm; it's between socioeconomic systems. Business, government, employees, customers, and society at large are partners. They form an organic, virtuous network in which each part is essential to the socioeconomic whole. Good education, healthcare, fair income distribution, cultural diversity, and a clean environment are essential to competitiveness. In short, the glocal economy will be dominated by social partners who cooperate to boost the economic health of the total system.

Customers and employees increasingly expect companies to espouse and stand for certain social principles. As **Spiegel**'s Hank Johnson asserts:

*To ignore civic responsibility is to ignore the mutually beneficial relation-
ship between you and the market.*

Mutually beneficial relations will best be achieved through:
- Long-Term Glocal Vision;
- Core Values;
- Environmental Ethics; and
- Socioeconomic Responsibility.

Long-Term Glocal Vision
Glocal companies envision themselves as part of an organic market system.
Again, it is **Sony**'s Morita who observes:
*The global market system is more and more a single interacting glocal
organism.*

Matsushita captures the glocal marketing paradigm in its company song which
inspires a shared mission:
*To send a stream of goods to the people of the world, like water gushing
from a fountain.*

Perhaps the best long-term vision comes from **Fujitsu**, the Japanese computer
giant. It stresses "cooperation and mutual prosperity, drawing on the best of the
cultures and customs of the world's people."
Its overall theme is: *What mankind can dream, technology can create.* Lew
Frauenfelder, president of **Fujitsu America** observes:
*We're merging core technologies to create 21s-century wonder products.
Success takes people who understand local needs and turn technology into
solutions. We will provide products tailored to how people want to live.*

On its 50th Anniversary in 1985, **Fujitsu** declared:
*In the next half century we'll automate offices and factories all over the Earth
and bring the miracle of electronics and new info-services into the home.
We'll help turn the world we've known into the place we'd like it to be.*

Core Values
Such a glocal vision draws on solid core values such as those at **Pepsi-Cola**,
Northern Telecom, and **Hewlett-Packard** *(see box overleaf).*

CORE VALUES

PEPSI-COLA

- **Teamwork**: *Work on real needs; combine functional excellence to produce exceptional results.*
- **Diversity**: *Value and promote differences of race, nationality, gender, age, background, experience, and style.*
- **Honesty**: *Speak openly and directly, with care and compassion; work hard to understand and resolve issues.*
- **Integrity**: *We do what we say.*

NORTHERN TELECOM

- **Customers:** *Create superior value for customers.*
- **People:** *Our people are our strength.*
- **Teamwork:** *Share one vision; we are one team.*
- **Innovation:** *Embrace change, reward innovation.*
- **Excellence:** *Our only standard.*
- **Commitment:** *We do what we say we will do.*

HEWLETT-PACKARD

- **Trust and respect:** *... for all our people.*
- **Personal achievement:** *... within teamwork contribution.*
- **Flexibility:** *... and continuous innovation.*
- **Leadership:** *... in technical quality and customer service*
- **Uncompromising integrity:** *... in all business aspects.*
- **Solid community contributions:** *... wherever we operate.*

(Sources: Relative company reports, documents)

Such customer-driven values underpin a visionary commitment both to excel and to be socially responsible within their local communities.

Environmental Ethic

Visionary firms also commit to help restore the planet's environment, as shown by the "green" efforts already noted.

But **The Body Shop** was started on the very basis of social responsibility and a "green" commitment. Founded by Anita Roddick, whom I call a *socialistic* *entrepreneur*, the firm is built on "high-virtue" policies such as *"save the earth"* and *"no cruelty to animals."* Its cosmetics are developed without animal testing, and packages and gift bags are made from biodegradable water hyacinth and banana leaves.

Through a *Trade not Aid* program, the firm seeks to protect plants and animal species as well as help indigenous peoples survive by:
• Buying Brazil nut oil from Kayapo Indians in the Brazilian rainforest to help the ecosystem survive;
• Trading with Nepalese paper makers to help save the endangered lokta shrub through use of local alternatives;
• Running a *Stop the Burning* campaign to publicize the plight of the rainforest.

Ben & Jerry's, the Vermont-based ice-cream and frozen yogurt maker, is a similar *socialistic entrepreneurial* firm. With a credo of *Turning Values Into Value*, it is the only firm in the world with a Director of Social Mission Development. Part of the mission is to *"improve the quality of life of a broad community — local and global"* with many initiatives *(see box below)*.

Socioeconomic Responsibility
Today, with the world in critical transition, the glocal community needs to solve common problems and set a new course.

BEN & JERRY'S "GLOCAL" COMMUNITY INITIATIVES

• The firm puts 7.5% of pretax earnings into a special foundation for "projects which are models of social change" and, in 1993 alone, gave more than $700,000.

• For each pint of ice cream sold, retailers also commit to donate 35-cents to a local organization.

• Ice-cream shops act as locations for voter registration sign-ups, offering a free cone to everyone who registers.

• The firm's *Peace Pop* ice-cream-on-a-stick is packed with a message *1% for Peace*, with 1% of profit promoting peace.

• All profit from *Rainforest Crunch* (made from cashews and Brazil nuts) go to develop nut-processing factory co-ops owned and operated by Brazilian rainforest communities.

Business alone cannot solve socioeconomic problems. But, as Peter Drucker asserts in *Post-Capitalist Society*, it's futile to argue that the *only* responsibility of business is to make profit. That's just its *first* duty. After all, a loss-making firm is socially irresponsible; it wastes scarce resources. Only profitable firms have a base from which to perform social good.

Above all, business must press for a redefinition of capitalism. It should present a new, dynamic vision of the socioeconomic system and how it ought to operate. This is best achieved by giving back to society some of the financial largess that it has bestowed on you.

One firm committed to democratic capitalism *and* societal progress is **Magna**, the auto parts maker led by Frank Stronach, another *socialistic entrepreneur*. With a culture based on "fair" — rather than "free" — enterprise, worker participation, and community orientation, its aims are spelled out in a unique *Corporate Constitution*. This stipulates that, of pretax profits:

- 10% must go to *"employee shareholders"*;
- 2% must go to charitable, cultural, educational, and political institutions *"to support the basic fabric of society"*; and
- 6% must go to foster *"long-term entrepreneurialism"* across the company.

As Lester Thurow avers in *Head to Head*, such communitarian systems with long-term goals will always defeat go-it-alone systems because they are demonstrably more competitive.

Checklist for "Glocal" Marketers

To succeed in the late-1990s and beyond, business leaders need an inspiring vision which captures the flow of the glocal market and embraces the four core values of the new age:

Passionate Caring
- Adopt an info-network, team-based structure.
- Scrap hierarchy and collapse the organization structure into a "cellular honeycomb" info-net design.
- Abandon functional, geographic, and product management in favor of customer-type management.
- Form self-directed teams around core competencies, or around customer-focused processes in the value chain, or around groups of customer types.
- Empower employees to *"do the unexpected"* and always exceed customer needs with *"honored guest"* service that *"comes from the heart"* and so *"can't be faked."*

- Create **Saturn**-like self-directed workteams that do their own work flow and human resource planning and management, and measure their own performance.
- Create a one-stop *"Liaison Group"* for customer groups.

Powerful Communication
- Use customer-driven info-nets to shrink home office staff levels, cut management layers, and coordinate activity as close to the customer as possible.
- Create a "virtual network" that cannot be beaten on time and convenience.

Cooperating to Compete
- Share information to multiply its value and gain network externalities.
- Forge RD&E, production, and cross-marketing strategic alliances with competitors to tap glocal markets in NAFTA and across the world.

Societal Commitment
- Develop core values that position the company as one firmly committed to societal values, globally and locally.
- Create a *socialistic entrepreneurial* mindset throughout the company and commit to community initiatives that augment your company's image in the eyes of your customers.
- How about articulating a dramatic 50-year corporate vision (yes, 50 years) that taps into the natural "flow" of the future glocal marketplace?

With such an inspired vision of the glocal market paradigm and a culture so committed to exceed future customer expectations, any company will develop a successful marketing mix, explored next in Step Five.

REVAMP
THE MARKET MIX
(New 4-Ps)

Mass marketing is obsolete.
This is due to changing households, complex technology-based
products, new ways to shop and pay, intense competition,
additional channels, and declining advertising effectiveness.
Personal marketing is what customers want.

—Jeff Snedden, VP Personal Marketing, **McCaw Cellular**

The Industrial Age of pure mass — of mass production, mass marketing, mass merchandising, mass advertising, and mass consumption — is over, finito! In tune with the *Global Village* metaphor, marketers must "glocalize" their brand mix to meet precise, individual customer needs.

The conventional 4-Ps (Product, Place, Price, and Promotion) must move beyond mass marketing myths to become:

  1. "Mass-Customized" Product (Beyond Homogenization)
  2. AnyTime + AnyPlace (Beyond Linear Channels)
  3. Total Value Price (Beyond Discount Pricing)
  4. Precise (1:1) Positioning (Beyond Mass Promotion)

1. "Mass-Customized" Product (Beyond homogenization)

"Only milk should be homogenized."

—Ad copy for *Lexus* automobile, **Toyota**

I'm sure you agree that people are more unique than products. And, having read to this point, I'm sure you'll also agree there are few (if any!) universal products.

Glocal companies don't make products with universal appeal but products with unique appeal for each customer. To develop *Lexus*, **Toyota** asked upper-income buyers what they valued in a vehicle. It then reverse-engineered the car and, at first launch, sales went into high orbit.

Even so-called "universal" products do not make global exceptions to the new glocal rule. After all, **Mercedes Benz** customizes luxury cars for both single owners and rental car fleets. Even in the general auto market, there is no "global car." **Nissan**, for example, develops basic "lead country" models which it *"carefully tailors"* to the dominant and distinct needs of provincial markets. It then *"further adapts"* them to local market needs. **Ford** also makes different cars with different option packages for regional markets in North America.

Not only do universal products need customizing, even "commodities" may need changing. Though a microchip may be a global product, its marketing mix must be glocal. And though food is generic and universal, individual commodity foods vary widely. For example, there are numerous varieties of rice. And each tastes different depending on where and how it was cultivated and cooked. In sum, even a grain of rice is glocal.

If you're still skeptical, please consider the numerous everyday products listed in the accompanying boxes.

Still, more needs to be said about this in specific reference to the "Product" element of the marketing mix. Product should be viewed in glocal terms. Only glocal thinking will result in products suitably adapted to diversifying consumer tastes. An effective "Product" element of the marketing mix depends on:

- "Mass Customization";
- Share of Customer (not Share of Market);
- Customer Managers (not Product Managers); and
- "Glocal" Segmentation.

"Mass Customization"

Most businesses pitch their products to the greatest number of users. But selling *more* goods to *fewer* people is more efficient.

Discovering that mass production is a major cause of declining competitiveness, innovative companies are rapidly embracing "mass customization" to gain the freedom to create greater variety and individuality in products. For example:

- **McGraw-Hill** delivers custom-made classroom textbooks in quantities under 100 copies;
- **Motorola** makes any one of 29 million varieties of pagers within 20 minutes of order;
- **Getaway Vacations** offers custom-designed tours to individuals at the price of group tour packages.

Glocal companies thus focus on one customer at a time. For example, **Second Skin** and other swimwear stores use a system designed by **Software Sportswear** to custom-tailor swimsuits to a woman's body shape. Wearing an "off-the-rack" garment, the system's digital camera projects her image onto a computer screen where the store clerk uses a stylus to mark adjustments to the fit, creating a perfectly snug garment. The customer then selects any of 150+ patterns and styles. After each selection, the screen reimages her in a precisely fitting swimsuit of the chosen fabric. Once a final choice is made, the garment is sewn up and delivered within a week.

Glocal companies thus manage customers not products and build "share of customer" not share of market.

"MASS CUSTOMIZATION" OF EVERYDAY PRODUCTS
— Food —

• Soup

Campbell Soup once failed in launching condensed soup in Britain by not explaining the need to add water. Consumers either thought the soup expensive or didn't want to make "watered-down" soup. In Quebec and Brazil, the soup failed because homemakers adamantly prefer to make their own. **Campbell** later launched soups that appeal to distinctly regional tastes: a fiery *Crema de Chile Poblano* soup in Mexico; *Flaki*, a peppery tripe soup in Poland; watercress/duck-gizzard soup in Hong Kong and China. Other products for the Chinese market include radish and carrot soup, pork/fig/date soup, and a scallop broth. The firm also is grabbing the Chinese market in North America with English-Chinese bilingual labeling.

• Gravy Cubes

A bouillon cube takes on many shapes and flavors around the world and also comes as a powder. In the United States, Germany, or Switzerland it's sold in chicken or beef flavors. In Mexico, it comes in tomato or shrimp flavor, as a corn bouillon in Argentina, chili in Kenya, mutton in Ireland, and pork in Thailand.

• "Glocal" Private Label

Loblaw's private label, *President's Choice*, has "glocalized" through global product-line extensions. Within three months, *Memories of Kobe* tamari garlic marinade outsold every pourable salad dressing. *Memories of Szechwan* peanut sauce and dressing outsold ketchup — all sizes, all varieties. Success also came with *Memories of Hawaii* beef short ribs, *Memories of Kobe* premarinated hamburger patties, *Memories of Ancient Damascus* tangy pomegranate sauce, and *Memories of Hong Kong* spicy black bean and garlic sauce.

These brands also allow well-traveled "Baby Boomers" to show their superior knowledge and make a statement about their taste and style. They can even feed their pets with *Gourmet Italian-Style Dog Food* — in either Cacciatore-style or Bolognese-style!

The label has pushed into global markets, being carried by **Wal-Mart** in the U.S., **K Mart** in Australia, **Park'N Shop** in Hong Kong, and other outlets in Sweden, South Africa, and the U.K. In short, this so-called "private" label has become a full-blown "glocal" brand.

"MASS-CUSTOMIZED" EVERYDAY PRODUCTS
— Fast Food —

"Glocal" Fast Food
To appeal to local tastes, global fast-food franchisors tailor product offerings and explain U.S. food items with photos on menu boards and place mats.

• **McDonald's**, under a *"Different tastes for different tastes"* slogan, often adds extra menu items to suit local taste:
    — France and Germany: wine and beer;
    — Italy: pasta salad;
    — Brazil: guarana berry soft drinks;
    — Hawaii: saimin (noodle soup) and rice;
    — Philippines: mixed spaghetti;
    — Malaysia/Singapore/Thailand: durian fruit milk shakes;
    — Japan: corn soup and teriyaki burgers;
    — Southern U.S.: chicken *fajitas* and *burritos*.

• **KFC** (Kentucky Fried Chicken) in Japan substitutes french fries for mashed potatoes and puts less sugar in coleslaw.

• **Olive Garden** (part of **General Mills**) has become the top Italian restaurant chain in North America (400+ outlets) by using 97 different menus that appeal to local palates. It also has 125 different local media plans and sponsors amateur sports, food festivals, and the arts in local communities.

Share of Customer (not Share of Market)
Rather than focusing on their overall marketing *scale*, modern marketers:
  • Focus on the *scope* of their long-term relationship with each customer.
  • Communicate directly *with* each customer rather than aiming/speaking *at* them in segments.
  • Cultivate a stream of *ongoing* business from each customer rather than grabbing groups of *one-time* buyers.
  • Focus on *"share of customer"* to build *overall* market share.

"MASS CUSTOMIZATION" OF EVERYDAY PRODUCTS
— Toiletries —

• Toothbrushes/Toothpaste/Shampoo
Johnson & Johnson developed the *Reach* toothbrush for the U.S. market, but "foreign" subsidiaries were free to decide the local market mix. In some cases, local preferences dictated a change in the brush. **P&G** tailors *all* products. While the desire for cavity-free teeth and healthy-looking hair are universal, company chairman Edwin Artzt says that culture demands product adaptation:
We must tailor products to fit customer needs based on culture, habits, preferred perfume, and hair and skin types.

• Razor Blades
In the 1980s, **Gillette** tried to *reverse* a natural glocal process where different brand names started to be used for razor blades, shampoos, and other products. Anxious to improve sales, local managers reformulated shampoo and varied ad copy. Head office reimposed globalization. Confused customers went elsewhere and profits spiralled downward and were only reversed by refocusing on local markets. Today, **Gillette** develops initial lines for entry into new markets using its traditional double-edged blade. If successful, its U.S. pens, deodorants, shampoos, and toothpastes are added. If problems arise, new products are created. In Mexico, for example, aerosol shaving cream was too expensive for people who shaved with soapy or plain water. So the firm launched *Prestobarba*, a cheaper shaving cream which was then rolled out across Latin America. *Black Silk* hair relaxer was taken from the African-American market into Africa at large.

• Cosmetics
Johnson Publishing, whose *Fashion Fair* is the [#]1 department store ethnic cosmetic brand, also makes *Eboné* skin care and makeup. **Revlon** has two ethnic cosmetics lines, *ColorStyle Collection* and *Darker Tones of Amay*. **Maybelline** markets a *Shades of You* line and runs an annual *"Shades of You Salute to You"* promotion to honor "unsung heroes" in black communities and donates to the *National Coalition of Black Women*. **Pavion** parlays its successful *Black Radiance* line into other ethnic arenas. Its *Solo Para Ti* (only for you) line is aimed at Hispanics and an African-American line is pending.

"MASS CUSTOMIZATION" OF EVERYDAY PRODUCTS
— Beverages —

• **Soft Drinks**

Coca-Cola, the world's [#]1 brand, varied the level of sweetener for each market. Even then, since many people still don't like *Coca-Cola*, the firm offers a variety of cola and other sodas. Granted, a year after *New Coke* (now *Coke II*) was launched, it was outsold by *Classic* ("old" *Coke*) by ten to one in most of North America. In the Great Lakes region, however, *New Coke* outsold *Classic* by a wide margin, again showing the wide variance in consumer tastes. Moreover, the success of **PepsiCo**'s equally diverse product line shows that neither *Coke* nor *Pepsi* are universal products.

• **Coffee**

Nestlé's coffee taste (and advertising) varies between markets. It long ago learned to blend different coffees for the British (who make it with milk) and the French (who like it black). To Canadians, "regular" coffee means "with cream and sugar," but to Americans this means "black." You can't sell coffee in Chile as you would in Germany. Chileans expect good coffee and buy on price while Germans pay any price for good coffee.

• **Beer**

Heineken beer is licensed and distributed in more than 160 countries. Although it's brewed to look and taste the same nearly everywhere, there are several notable exceptions. And whereas it's usually positioned as a high-class beer worth the extra cost, again there are many exceptions. In Britain, the beer is made with less alcohol than normal to match local taste and is promoted as a distinctive yet standard price beer. In France, ads are designed to entice a nation of wine drinkers to drink more beer. In America, it's positioned as a foreign status symbol. But at home in The Netherlands, this prestige brand is promoted as the standard price beer for everyone!

"Share of customer" firms realize that it costs five to ten times as much to attract a new customer as it does to keep an existing one. Since firms typically lose 25% of their customers a year, every 1% drop in that attrition rate boosts profits by at least 5%. Glocal firms thus look beyond short-term profits to the long-term earnings from each person's lifelong custom.

"MASS CUSTOMIZATION" OF EVERYDAY PRODUCTS
— Household Items —

• **Fridges**

Despite attempts to unite Europe, national tastes and regional markets remain strong. Northern Europeans want large fridges because they shop only once a week in supermarkets. Southern Europeans like small fridges because they pick through open-air markets almost every day. Moreover, northerners like the freezer compartment on the bottom, southerners on the top. And Britons, who devour frozen foods, insist on units with 60% freezer space. Appliance maker **Electrolux** thus offers 120 basic fridge designs with 1,500 variants. Observes president Leif Johansson:

I must be a good Frenchman in France and a good Italian in Italy. I go global only when I can, and stay local when I must.

• **Pens**

Parker Pen (now part of **Gillette**) was always known for higher-priced, superior-quality pens. In 1984, under attack from **Bic** and **Cross**, it embarked on an ill-fated mission to use the same products, pricing, packaging, and advertising worldwide. Aiming to be the world's [#]1 pen maker, it overlooked market nuances. Customers and employees resisted the global strategy. Indeed, the firm's ad agency, Ogilvy & Mather, repeatedly warned that globalization was a mistake!

• **Dolls**

Mattel's *Barbie* doll did very poorly in Japan until manufacturing rights were given to **Takara**, a Japanese toy and doll specialist. Most Japanese thought *Barbie*'s breasts were far too big, her legs much too long, and her eyes too blue. With brown eyes and a suitably modified body, the new *Barbie* found instant market success, selling 2 million units in two years.

• **Insect Spray**

S.C.Johnson & Sons customizes all products to meet regional differences. For *Raid* insect spray, the company first determined which bugs were the worst pests in various American markets. For example, while cockroaches are the most hated in New York and Houston, fleas are most trouble in Birmingham and Tampa. Of 18 regions targeted in this way, market share grew in 16 of them.

Customer Managers (not Product Managers)

To shift focus from share of market to share of customer, firms should manage customers not products, replacing product managers with customer portfolio managers. Customer managers should be charged with increasing each customer's lifetime value to the firm.

American Express, for example, had separate marketing departments for its *Gold Card, Optima Card, Platinum Card,* and basic *Personal Card.* Under this setup, card product managers ran their own programs, frequently in conflict with other card manager strategies. Since the company knew the personal card-use idiosyncracies of its 37 million customers, in 1992 it reassigned each customer to a *"loyalty group"* (such as frequent business travelers) under a customer marketing manager.

Customer managers can offer special features tailored to customer usage needs. For example, the frequent business traveler group can offer personally relevant services (such as paid car rental insurance, an emergency hotline, or restaurant guide) to each customer based on their existing pattern of card usage.

Even **P&G**, which made product management the marketing standard, has switched to customer managers who look after major supermarket chains. They coordinate *all* **P&G** products carried by each store of their particular chain, maximizing overall sales for that chain, not for each product itself.

"Glocal" Segmentation

In the glocal market, then, segmentation strategies need rethinking. Most firms see themselves as one of three types:

• **Product Specialist:** Making a standard product or narrow range of products for all segments across all geographic markets (e.g., running shoes for all consumers);

• **Market Specialist:** Making a standard product or wide range of products for one segment in all geographic markets (e.g., all types of footwear for children); or

• **Niche Specialist:** Making unique but standard products for one or more unique but standard segments across all geographic markets (e.g., running shoes for children).

These strategies pitch standard products to mythical homogeneous consumers in all markets *(left-hand side of diagram).*

This is where product globalization fails. For example, **Nike** used to be so technology- and product-driven that it misjudged the 1980s' aerobics market. Its aerobic shoe was functionally superior and sturdy but looked clunky against the sleek and attractive **Reebok** model. The market also rejected the style of a new casual shoe. These linear product-line extensions also blurred the firm's brand image and sales fell. Says founding chairman and CEO Phil Knight:

We used to think everything started in the lab. Now we realize everything spins off the consumer. The consumer has to lead product innovation.

In 1990 **Nike** set out to be *"the world's best sports and fitness company."* It talked and listened to men and women at amateur sporting events, in gyms, and on tennis courts. It spent time in retail stores, watching what happened across the counter.

As a result, the firm created separate brands and sub-brands. For basketball players, there are three sub-brands: *Air Jordon* for superior all-round players; *Force* for aggressive, muscular players; and *Flight* for fast players. For tennis players, *Challenge Court* appeals to the young, rebellious, anti-club type; *Supreme Court* is for the conservative type.

To create a separate brand for the casual shoe wearer, the firm bought **Cole-Haan**, the maker of dress shoes and accessories. With these changes, **Nike** restored profitability and commands 30% of the athletic shoe market.

As **Nike** learned, the market is full of glocal customers pursuing individual buying strategies. This creates a *brand-new* market paradigm. For the glocal era, a new segmentation strategy is essential:

• **"Glocal" Marketing:** Offering tailored products for numerous unique customers scattered across the glocal market horizon *(right-hand side of diagram)*.

In turn, these disparate customers must be reached via a multiplicity of channels, discussed next.

2. AnyTime + AnyPlace (Beyond linear channels)

You need to attract customers with preferences
different from those satisfied by regular outlets.
—Roger Stangeland, chairman, **Vons**

Channels must align with what customers need to know, how and where they want to buy, how and where they want service.   Channels are not merely conduits to sell something but are for serving individual buyers wherever they might be in the market. "Place" is where the customer is located, *not* where the retailer is located. And, with customers scattered across the market, "Place" becomes "AnyPlace."

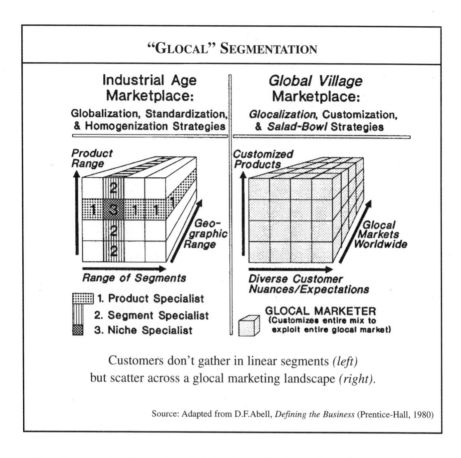

"GLOCAL" SEGMENTATION

Industrial Age Marketplace:
Globalization, Standardization, & Homogenization Strategies

Global Village Marketplace:
Glocalization, Customization, & Salad-Bowl Strategies

Product Range

Customized Products

Geo-graphic Range

Glocal Markets Worldwide

Range of Segments

Diverse Customer Nuances/Expectations

1. Product Specialist
2. Segment Specialist
3. Niche Specialist

GLOCAL MARKETER
(Customizes entire mix to exploit entire glocal market)

Customers don't gather in linear segments *(left)* but scatter across a glocal marketing landscape *(right)*.

Source: Adapted from D.F.Abell, *Defining the Business* (Prentice-Hall, 1980)

Glocal companies thus take a "whole channel" view of how to serve markets. "AnyTime+AnyPlace" channels involve:
- Satellite Site Selection;
- "Glocal" Retail Outlets;
- Dedicated Distribution Channels;
- Person-to-Person Channels;
- Touchscreen Kiosks;
- Telecom Channels; and
- "Green" Channels.

Satellite Site Selection
Geographic Info-Systems (GIS) let you pinpoint the optimum site for a retail or kiosk outlet.

Periodic high-resolution aerial photos, taken from satellites, reveal the population density, direction of growth, and traffic pattern of target market areas. *TIGER* (topologically integrated geographic encoding/referencing) is the U.S.

Census Bureau's powerful mapping system. It lets you map every store, branch, or home with exquisite precision. Using geographic coordinates (latitude and longitude) you can locate each home or place of business by its exact position along the street, not its local zip code. Indeed *(as asserted later under "Data-Base Marketing")*, zip codes are obsolete!

Typical users of such imagery, either in photo form or digitized for computer manipulation, are fast-food chains. **McDonald's** even has its own system, *Quintillion*, which it uses to plan new outlets and design local marketing campaigns. Most people decide to visit a restaurant only three to five minutes beforehand, and most sales come from three "traffic destinators." Those are homes, workplaces, or shops within a five-minute walk or drive. Hence, highly detailed market awareness is crucial.

McDonald's now sells its GIS system to ad agencies, supermarkets, auto dealers, movie chains, retailers, couriers, and banks. Computerized maps are far superior to zip code analysis. With a "spatial data base," a bank can physically "see" clients' homes on a computer screen. It can highlight households with savings accounts, mortgages (or overdrafts!), the location of banking machines, and competitors' branches — and much more about marketplace channels and product potentials.

Pepsi-Cola also uses GIS to pinpoint the best places for new *Pizza Hut, Taco Bell,* or *KFC* outlets. **Federal Express** uses it to site drop boxes and estimate how many trucks and planes are needed in peak periods. And **Conrail** keeps tabs on 20,000 miles of track with special track-monitoring cars which feed data into a GIS to alert engineers to maintenance needs. The company also uses GIS to identify new commercial customers near rail lines.

"Glocal" Retail Outlets

Such technology helps companies tailor their retail outlets to local neighborhoods.

McDonald's outlet in Darien (Conn.) is a mammoth tourist-focused outlet. It has 20 cash registers (including portables for overflow crowds), a 12-foot grill, 32 telephones, and a tourist center equipped with maps and ATM machines. **McDonald's** has also explored alliances with big oil companies to open outlets at gas stations. Tests of the concept include food stands inside convenience stores with gas pumps and a free-standing restaurant at a **Texaco** outlet. The chain also has struck a deal with **Wal-Mart** to convert snack bars in many of its stores to **McDonald's** outlets and is negotiating a similar deal with **Home Depot**. The firm also tested home delivery in 1993 and is expanding the service. It's also opening restaurants in hospitals and universities — even on airplanes: Its meals for kids are served by request on **United Airlines**' flights out of Chicago.

Sears also is tailoring its stores to local markets — even to airline travelers. Its Ala Moana store (HI) caters to Japanese tourists, providing an airline ticket outlet, a currency exchange service, and a one-hour photo service. The cosmetics section carries Japanese lines, and the store accepts *JCB* and *Saison* credit cards plus various Japanese "prepaid" cards.

The **Vons** supermarket chain always tailors its stores to the taste and make-up of local markets. Using customer surveys, computer-generated sales/inventory data, and localized research, it creates store formats to present a custom array of products for each neighborhood. The chain has also cloned the "price club" concept, with a separate *Expo* format of discounted goods. Another *Super Combo* format features a full-service bank, a party store with catering facilities, plus dry cleaner, one-hour photo store, pharmacy, and expanded grocery sections. To again quote chairman Roger Stangeland:

We get tighter market penetration with varied formats.

That's why specialty retailers such as **Home Depot**, **Foot Locker**, and **Toys "R" Us** have been doing well. They focus on the needs of loyal shoppers and offer enough diversity to cater to individual tastes. Their success is based on being right for every customer every time, differentiating each store and each line of goods to capitalize on different tastes.

Barnes & Noble also spoils bookbuyers with top-notch service, lots of chairs and benches, a coffee bar, and localized merchandise. **B&N**'s EVP of marketing, Steve Riggio, says:

In stocking a store we try to reflect the diversity and individuality of its market.

Dedicated Distribution Channels

Some firms use dedicated distribution networks to forge lasting customer relationships. The agri-products division of **American Cyanamid**, the pharma-chemical firm, has an *AgriCenter* network of 1,800 key dealers. But it treats the dealers as customers, putting the company closer to its end customers, farmers.

The centers buy products direct from **Cyanamid**, cutting out one level in the distribution chain and enhancing sales and technical support. The centers supply farmers with complete information on new products and hold educational meetings to discuss products and any related problems.

This dialogue alerted the company to a problem that arose during the severe droughts of the late 1980s. Some farmers suffered crop damage when a herbicide did not break down as it should due to the extremely dry conditions. **Cyanamid** used satellites to locate the crop damage and then sent its *AgriCenter* dealers and sales reps to visit each affected farm. This "high-touch/high-tech" approach led to a quick solution to the problem and further cemented customer relations.

Person-to-Person Channels

In many ways, multilevel companies (such as **Avon**, **Mary Kay**, or **Amway**) come closest to what is now called "personal marketing" *(discussed later under "Precise Positioning").* They offer convenience, personal attention, and in-home or at-work access to sample products. They build *global scope* through *local scale* representation. **Avon** divides the North American market into 900,000 territories of 100 homes each. It's even broken into the Chinese market, with thousands of factory workers promoting cosmetics to their comrades.

Such family-oriented relationship-marketing is so successful that **MCI**, the telecom carrier, contracts with **Avon** and **Amway** to market door-to-door its *Friends & Family* long-distance service. Still, despite a "close-to-the-customer" approach, multilevel firms are not glocal marketers, in three ways:

• For more and more North Americans, this way of selling is too high-pressure, inconvenient, and intrusive. As with telemarketing's ringing phone, the "ding-dong" of the doorbell interrupts the "high-tech" activity of people engrossed in the new wizardry of their *"Electronic Cottage."* And selling at the office interrupts work. The more intrusive the marketing, the more people will slam the phone in your ear or the door in your face.

• To be fair, **Avon**'s catalog now has a growing selection of products (for men as well as women) and more upscale cosmetics and fragrances. It also has hair-care products for African-Americans and a Spanish-language catalog for Hispanics/Latinos. Beyond this, however, these companies do not mirror the market with a multiethnic salesforce. And although they know their geographic markets and potential customers intimately, they don't tailor products to neighborhood markets.

• Neither are these firms very "high-tech." Products are presented in a standard catalog of mostly standard fare. It's either "take it" or "leave it." And there is too much paperwork. The catalog should have electronic channel access and ordering options for those buyers who want them. And, to boost reliability and speed delivery, the salesforce should carry laptops to enter and track orders — and then transmit them by fax or satellite.

Touchscreen Kiosks
More than 100,000 interactive kiosks — *excluding* bank ATMs or lottery machines — were in use across America by the end of 1993 (up from 62,000 in 1992).

They perform a variety of retail and service delivery tasks *(see boxes on next two pages).*

KIOSK CHANNELS
— Retail Outlets —

• **MicroMall** kiosks use compact disks to present text, graphics, and audio. The kiosks have computer hard drives and modems, so product info can be changed whenever needed, giving retailers an advantage over printed catalogs. **JCPenney**, **Spiegel**, and **Hammacher-Sclemmer** are already on line and other retailers such as **Lands' End** will be added soon. They can change the copy, price, or photo of a product, or can add or delete products at will. The ultimate goal is to bring this technology in-home over the TV. For now, 20 kiosks are operating in Chicago hotels and office buildings, with expansion into New York, California, and Ohio imminent. The kiosks take the customer through a selection process: store-to-department-to-product. The same technology also is behind a test of electronic telephone listings, including animated ads in the yellow pages. **Bell Atlantic**, which developed the software with **MicroMall**, is putting portable players in 300 homes in North Virginia. They contain 1 million residential and 250,000 business phone listings.

• In 1993, **K Mart** launched the first national retail network of kiosks in Canada — one for each of its 124 stores. The kiosks dispense coupons on featured sale items and show customers where these products can be found in the store. The directory on each kiosk is customized according to each store's particular layout. The unit has a touchscreen and, responding to a shopper's prompts, displays various coupon offers. When selected, the coupon is printed and dispensed. During the print operation, the kiosk also delivers advertising and promo messages. The kiosks allow **K Mart** to give extra discount on featured items. But their main advantage is a substantial boost in sales — by as much as 25% on kiosk-couponed items. They encourage shoppers to visit more areas of the store, possibly buying extra items they would not otherwise see.

• **IBM** is marketing *Ultimedia* interactive kiosk directories for retail and deli stores, as well as for bridal and gift registries. Its *InfoFood* supermarket kiosk provides coupons, store directories, recipes, food preparation tips, and new product information. An *InfoSpirits* version, featuring store/product directories and anti-drinking/driving messages, is being tested by Pennsylvania state liquor stores.

KIOSK CHANNELS
— AnyPlace Service —

• The U.S. **Postal Service** is rolling out 10,000 *Postal Buddy* kiosks so people can register address changes and label packages without going to the clerk's window.

• **California**'s state office of information technology is testing kiosks that update car registrations, search for birth certificates, and handle other state business.

• **Ontario** has a pilot project using IBM kiosks for renewing auto license plate stickers and paying traffic fees (or fines!) by credit card.

• Car dealers in Toronto are using an interactive *AutoShopper* kiosk of **AutoData Marketing Systems**. Shoppers can compare options, competing dealership leasing and service policies, and even find out if a given assembly line can build their dream car.

• The **Minnesota Twins** baseball team tested kiosks in 1992 and put 30 units in stores and malls during the 1993 season.

• **Neuberger Museum of Art** (Purchase, NY) uses kiosks to show videos of artists or critics talking about a painting you've just seen.

• **Intouch**'s *i.Station* touchscreen kiosk lets music buyers sample 32,000 CDs via headphones. Activated by a bar-coded plastic card, the kiosk provides liner notes, reviews, and titles of other releases by artist and genre.

Telecom Channels

While product delivery channels will always vary, telecom links will rise to the forefront because they offer the easiest and cheapest way for buyer and seller to interact.

In banking, for example, the trend toward electronic channels is clear from more and more kiosk applications *(see box opposite)* and the following table.

BANKING TRANSACTIONS BY DELIVERY CHANNEL

	1985	1993	2004
PCs	0.1%	0.2%	3.0%
Phones	3.0%	8.8%	18.0%
ATMs/ETKs	26.1%	36.2%	48.0%
Branches	70.8%	54.8%	31.0%

(Sources: American Bankers' Assn. for historical data; 2004 forecast by Glocal Marketing Inc.)

KIOSK CHANNELS
— ATMs and ETKs —

• Expanded ATM Services

Texas Commerce Bank's new ATM system lets customers get monthly statements, transfer funds, stop payments on checks, apply for ATM cards, review accounts, and get information on interest rates and various bank products. Future ATMs will offer satellite-fed interactive video, taking deposits from anywhere, helping arrange loans — and, yes, even issuing coupons and airline tickets. **Automatic Coupon** has launched *Automatic Bank Bonus*, a delivery system that issues discount coupons for well-known products with the ATM transaction record. Banks using the system include **First Tennessee**, **First Interstate**, **First Chicago**, and **Marine Midland**. Firms issuing coupons include **McDonald's**, **Pepsi**, and **Bally's**.

• Electronic Transaction Kiosks (ETKs)

Air travelers can now phone reservations to an airline or travel agent and then go to a nearby ETK, insert a credit/debit card, and the ETK will print and dispense the tickets on the spot. ETKs will be in office buildings, hotel lobbies, airports, and other high-traffic sites. Firms setting up ETK networks include **Airline Computer Tickets**, **Mail Boxes**, and **QDAT**. More than 12,000 ETKs are expected to be in place by 1998. Travel agents pay $9 for each ticket sent via a kiosk — less than the cost of express mail or courier. Future travelers will be able to write their own tickets. Agents, who book 85% of airline seats, are in danger of being bypassed by ETKs which could handle 25% of all bookings by 1998. While it will be tough to plan vacations with ETKs, **American Airlines**' *Sabre* system soon will be a "global travel agency," handling every type of vacation booking. The days of the travel agent may be numbered.

Firms also use telephone "Call Centers." While these are used for what is called telemarketing, tele-*selling* to consumers (as opposed to industrial buyers) will become obsolete due to its intrusiveness. Citing no lesser authority than the marketing VP of **McCaw Cellular** (now part of **AT&T**), Jeff Snedden:

The declining efficiency of consumer-rejected technology leads to more technology, still greater customer rejection, and demands for regulation.

The best "Call Centers" are *user*-driven, providing individualized access worldwide through multiple 800/900-number access points at no incremental cost. **Chevron** thus operates a 24-hour help-line for its 9,000 service stations across North America to help them solve gas pump, point-of-sale terminals, or modem problems. **Polaroid** uses them to serve those family and business clients who want to be served that way, tracking sales to calculate the lifetime value of each customer. **Corel** markets its popular *CorelDRAW* software through local distributors and dealers, coordinating them electronically via "Call Centers." **Dell**'s customers order computers direct and software users call **WordPerfect** for on-line help via a "Call Center."

Pizza companies deliver 500 million pizzas a year in the United States and Canada via "Call Center" phone banks and a patchwork of local drivers. Gourmet restaurants turn to local services such as **Takeout Taxi** to deliver full-course meals to homes. And **Shoppers Express** runs a national service for customers calling in grocery orders. In each case, a "Call Center" routes each request to a local supermarket for home delivery — much as long-distance florist services operate.

Channels also are shifting toward desktop computers — and not just to place orders. This is because any product which can be digitized can be sold, delivered, and serviced electronically. Bill McKiernan, CEO of **McAffee**, a software developer, sums it up this way:

For any product that starts out in electronic form (such as computer software) it makes no sense to download it onto disks, wrap them up in cardboard and plastic, weigh them down with a three-pound user manual, then ship them out to customers who then copy the disks to their own harddrive. Instead, we can download it to their computer directly and instantly.

The volume of shopping over electronic channels is exploding. Overall, the potential tele-shopping market is huge. Consider what we now spend on related services:

- $80 billion a year through catalogs;
- $80 billion a year for local phone service;
- $16 billion a year to rent home videos; and
- $6 billion a year on video games.

Hence, beyond the examples in *"Shopping in 2004"* at the front of this book, all progressive retailers are opening electronic outlets. **Macy's** put a *TVMacy's* shopping channel on the air in 1994. **Nordstrom** has a similar channel and **JCPenney** participates in several new ITV shopping channels.

Of course, nondigitizable products, however they are bought and distributed, do require packaging. This raises the matter of points of recycle and "Green" Channels.

"Green" Channels

Packaging is a necessary evil. It prevents products from being spoiled or damaged and often is simply essential to convenient use. However, responsible marketers are stripping away useless packaging and switching to flexible packaging such as plastic pouches.

Flexible packaging needs less resources and energy to make, fewer energy-consuming trucks to transport, less refrigeration and storage, and less landfill space *(see box, below)*. Indeed, flexible packaging is landfill-safe because it releases no toxic chemicals, explosive gases, or other pollutants. Moreover, having a higher energy value, when flexible packaging is incinerated it generates more fuel with less combustible wastes.

FLEXIBLE "GREEN-PACK" PACKAGE REDESIGN			
	Effective Reductions		
Product Redesign	Package	Product	Landfill
(From ⟶ To)	Volume	Weight	Space
Soup:			
Steel can ⟶ Pouch	97%	93%	57%
Milk:			
Paper carton ⟶ Pouch	93%	80%	92%
Diapers:			
Folding carton ⟶ Bag	86%	85%	31%
Fabric Softener:			
Plastic bottle ⟶ Pouch	84%	85%	74%
Drinks:			
Glass bottle ⟶ Pouch	82%	96%	49%
Glass bottle ⟶ Carton	70%	90%	37%
Coffee:			
Steel ban ⟶ Brick pack	55%	70%	15%

(Source: Flexible Packaging Association, based on 1992 recycling rates)

Flexible packaging smoothes out distribution handling, eases store display and consumer use, and is environmentally sound. Examples include the following:
- **Anheuser-Busch** shortened beer cans by 1/8th of an inch, cutting aluminum usage by 20 million pounds per year.
- **S.C. Johnson** repackaged *Agree Plus* shampoo in a stand-up pouch to use 80% less plastic.
- **Colgate-Palmolive**'s stand-up toothpaste tube slashed packaging/shipping material by 70%.
- **P&G** "concentrated" its powdered and liquid *Tide*, *Cheer*, and other detergents, reducing paperboard and plastic used in containers by 50% and 20% respectively.
- **P&G** eliminated outer cartons from *Secret* and *Sure* deodorant, reducing paperboard use by 3.4 million pounds per year.
- **General Mills** thinned down the liner-bag inside cereal boxes by 12%, saving 500,000 pounds of plastic a year.

Some companies also help consumers to recycle products, setting up "points of recycle" channels.

Nike has a recycling program called *Reuse-a-Shoe* for old sneakers, even those made by competitors. Shoppers get a $5-$10 rebate for each pair returned to bins placed in footwear stores by **Nike**'s *Environmental Action Team (EAT)*. The company tears up and granulates the shoes, giving the rubber, leather, and nylon to **Atlas Track & Tennis** which turns the materials into running tracks.

Similarly, **Aveda**, a maker of botanically based hair/skin care products, helps shoppers recycle bottlés and tubes through its *Earth Action* program, collecting them at beauty salons.

Finally, of course, distribution channels also are channels of communication, for gathering feedback from the marketplace. That's the ultimate in marketplace recycling.

Hence, the lifeblood of a futuristic company is marketplace information.

The glocal firm's computerized info-network needs to be all-knowing; the nucleus around which the marketing mix revolves. Like a hologram, it will contain precise knowledge about all customers in the firm's marketing universe. A boundaryless yet detailed mass of market knowledge, it will be what Marshall McLuhan called *"a total field of inclusive awareness."*

Although massive and constantly changing, this info-base selforganizes to reveal glocal consumer patterns — "AnyTime, AnyPlace."

We'll return to this topic under *"Data-Base Marketing."*

Meanwhile, marketplace information also is essential to effective value pricing, discussed next.

3. Total Value Price (Beyond Discount Pricing)

Day in, day out, we see no success with coupons.
It's such a nonsense way of doing business. It's like
having artificial prices and then knocking 20%-30% off.
We want a less complicated, simpler world.

—Durk Jager, Executive VP, **Procter & Gamble**

After the "Mini-Depression," as we move into the "Super-Boom," the ongoing customer search for total value will be met by a blend of solid pricing and branding:

- "No-Dicker" Pricing;
- Every Day Low Pricing (EDLP);
- Electronic Couponing;
- "Blue-Chip" Branding;
- "Glocal" Pricing; and
- Ownership Benefits.

"No-Dicker" Pricing

People are sick of uncertain prices, regardless of the type of product. Instead of dickering over price, automakers are finally wooing buyers with option-loaded models at factory-set fixed prices, a strategy they call "value pricing."

Saturn (part of **GM**) was first to move away from buyer incentives and price haggling, quoting fixed prices for all cars. Now, **GM** is pushing "one-price" retailing company wide. When it extended value pricing to the 11-year-old *Chevy Cavalier* for 1993, sales soared 26%. Value-priced *Pontiac Sunbird* and *Buick LeSabre* expanded their sales by 19% and 15% in the same period. The new high-end *Olds Aurora* is being sold the same way. Indeed, **GM** says value pricing will be the cornerstone of future marketing plans throughout its lineup.

Ford adopted a fixed "one-price" strategy for its *Escort* model in 1992. The concept was so popular that the company extended it to the *Thunderbird* and *Mercury Cougar* for 1993, boosting sales by 55% and 37% respectively! Observes Ross Roberts, VP-GM of *Ford Division*:

We're simply selling cars the way consumers have told us they want to buy those cars.

Every Day Low Pricing (EDLP)

Begun by **Wal-Mart**, "every day low pricing" (EDLP) creates price stability, cuts advertising costs, builds an image of reliability and fairness — and boosts retailer profit. Based on 1992 results, the most profitable supermarket chains use EDLP while high/low pricers earn meager profit margins:

Top 5 EDLP Chains		Top 5 High/Low Chains	
Albertson's	2.7%	Giant Foods	2.0%
Food Lion	2.5%	Vons	1.3%
Hannaford	2.4	American Stores	1.2%
Bruno's	2.2%	Safeway	0.7%
Winn Dixie	2.1%	Kroger	0.5%

(Source: Ryan Management Group)

For producers, as the 1980s showed, price promotions devalue brand equity. That's why, in 1992, **P&G** scrapped promotional discounts that led customers to expect ever-lower prices. To restore brand equity, the company adopted a "value pricing" strategy worldwide. Trade promotion budgets were slashed, shifting money into advertising and new product development.

P&G also wants to be rid of paper coupons. It has reduced couponing by 17% in each of the last two years to slash costs. Coupons appeal to consumers who have no propensity to be loyal. **P&G** is using EDLP to redirect money away from disloyal coupon-clippers to its loyal user base. The goal is to rebuild the brand loyalty **P&G** enjoyed until the early 1970s when inflation hit the economy. Now, with inflation back down to minimal levels, price competition will intensify. By the late 1990s, **P&G**'s pricing strategy will have great buyer appeal as "blue-chip" brands *(discussed below)* come back in vogue.

Electronic Couponing
Future coupons will be electronic and personalized.

In 1993, about 1.5 billion coupons were dispensed automatically at supermarkets by **Catalina**'s *Checkout Direct* instant coupon printers. As groceries pass over the checkout barcode scanner, the printer dispenses coupons for either competing brands or complementary products — based on what was just bought!

This lets firms such as **P&G**, **Kraft,** or **Quaker Oats** take aim at a single buyer, with surgical precision, in real-time, at the point of sale, marketwide. That's real-time one-to-one (1:1) positioning based on real-time 1:1 market research.

Catalina checkout coupon printers now are installed in more than 5,500 stores. A. C. Nielsen says 9.4% of the coupons are eventually redeemed, compared with only 2.5% of freestanding coupons clipped from newspaper ads. Nevertheless, that's still a lot of waste paper. **Pepsi-Cola** has stopped using the service until it evaluates whether it brings in enough new customers to warrant the expense. They cost seven cents each to issue versus one cent for regular coupons.

Advanced Promotion Technologies (APT), 24% owned by **P&G** and 10% by **Vons** the supermarket chain, operates *Vision Value Network*. This checkout device also dispenses coupons, plays short commercials on a video screen, and offers credit or debit cards to serve as frequent-shopper cards. The program boosted market share by 9% for participating brands in the chain. The point-of-purchase system also delivers personalized offer letters to consumers at the checkout, saving postal and production costs.

"Blue-Chip" Branding

With their coupon barrages and price discounts, brand managers have trained consumers to shop for goods on price. Private-label products now represent 18% of unit volume. Some people expect them to account for up to 25% of volume by 1998 and eventually as much as 50%. Their growth in cereals, cheese, diapers, soft drinks, and cigarettes has been spectacular. Retailer profit on private-label products is typically 50%-100% higher than on national brands.

Private-label products now account for more than 50% of all discount house sales. Discount houses are expected to use high-margin/low-cost private-label foods to try to dominate the retail food market in the next 10 years. Warehouse stores will soon be adding more private-label items to differentiate themselves from competitors and to stimulate sales.

On the other hand, private labels really are a phenomenon of the "Mini-Depression." While shoppers will still seek out value as the "Super-Boom" takes off, discounters will lose out as people return to quality retailers and established brands.

Meanwhile, to win against wholesale clubs, supermarkets should concentrate on what they do better: service, quality, convenience, and custom-tailored local neighborhood offerings.

A shakeout of superfluous line extensions and private labels is already under-way. Indeed, the "blue-chip" brands are unscathed. For example, these [#]1 brand-name products of 1923 were still tops, 70 years later, in 1993:

• **Campbells**	Soup
• **Coca-Cola**	Soft drinks
• **Del Monte**	Canned food
• **Kodak**	Film
• **GE**	Appliances
• **Gillette**	Razors
• **Goodyear**	Tires
• **Ivory (P&G)**	Soap
• **Nabisco**	Biscuits
• **Wrigley**	Chewing gum

Once the ridiculous product overchoice situation is trimmed down, the supermarket of the future will carry a smaller section of genuinely high-quality, high-value brands. Their "blue-chip" equity restored, brands will again fetch high prices.

This should not be surprising. Forced to cut through brand clutter, consumers have become perceptive in distinguishing real value. Few marketers succeed in presenting the salient attributes of new products — the notable exception being *President's Choice* which has become a "blue chip" brand in its own right. Amid the clutter, consumers rarely see new products as "new." They have become numb to newness. Hence, is it really any wonder that 70% of "new" products fail!

"Glocal" Pricing

As Japanese firms have found, glocal businesses know best how consumers perceive value. Company-wide info-exchange of cost structures allow them to optimize global pricing while responding to local market needs.

As noted earlier, the pricing strategy of Japanese firms is market-driven not profit-driven. Starting from desired local market share, they estimate what price will achieve that share, and push down costs so the market-based price is viable. They are so good at this that weaker competitors accuse them of "dumping." I repeat, they're glocal marketing!

The old marketing wisdom was that the price of a product sold "abroad" must be *higher* than that of the same product sold "at home." This was true only when multinationals shipped across the world and through tariff barriers. For the borderless, info-networked glocal firm in the era of global free trade, such problems vanish. It can "glocalize" its cost structure and offer products at prices in line with local buying power and local competitor prices.

Ownership Benefits

True value is increasingly info-based. After all, information is money. And info-intensive products delivered info-intensively will raise brand equity and command superior prices. Hence the success of courier companies.

Emphasizing overall product benefits shifts the focus from price-cutting to value-priced brand equity — the exact opposite of what firms did in the 1980s. Instead of asking "How *price* sensitive are customers?" firms should ask the reverse: "How *benefit* sensitive are customers to *extra* brand performance?"

Value thus goes beyond warranties on product quality. In the 1990s, "high value" doesn't mean high quality at a high price. Neither does it mean low prices if that means low-grade quality. So prices should be consistent and fully explained. **Irvine Ranch Market**, for example, finds that people will pay extra for locally grown and organic produce because it's fresh-picked. Its meat is also fresh-cut by a butcher who's always on duty. And it clearly labels "diet" and "organic" foods which then outsell competing brands by two-to-one.

People are strategic consumers. They seek value — the best quality to suit their needs — at every price level. They don't want prestige if that's seen as snobbish or self-indulgent. People no longer buy to impress others but to own personally satisfying products. They just want a fair price as part of a "total value" package. That's the new prestige.

"Total Value Price" thus stresses fringe benefits or *Purchase Perks*. For instance, **Toyota** dealers telephone *Lexus* owners to remind them about servicing — and offer to send a chauffeur to pick up the car. **Nissan** uses an outside consultant to phone *Infiniti* owners after each service visit — to ask how they were treated. Customer-driven auto dealers also give a free wash, polish, and wax to each car that's in for service.

By committing to the "total value" of the "ownership experience," these companies transcend similarities in price and quality. Indeed, car warranty restrictions are typically ignored by Japanese car dealers. They usually fix defects at no cost during the car's life.

Reasoning that a car's warranty should protect the owner not the factory, **Nissan** even provides a rescue service if you are dumb enough to lock your keys in the car! How's that for "total value" pricing?

4. Precise Positioning (Beyond Mass Advertising)

> *Our goal is to return marketing to the 19th century,*
> *a time when merchants knew their customers by name.*
>
> —Robert Perkins, VP Marketing, **Pizza Hut**

Just as "Product," "Place," and "Price" must be tailored to individual customer needs, so must "Promotion" — which now should be called "Precise (1:1) Positioning."

As such, mass advertising is obsolete. It must evolve with the times and find a new future. Consider the evolution since the 19th century:

• **Agricultural-age merchants never advertised**. They didn't need to. Even after local newspapers came along, most advertising was "word of mouth." Merchants came to know each customer one-to-one, learning their personal idiosyncracies. Lifetime relationship marketers, they carried customer data in their heads.

   They cultivated each shopper's ongoing business, seeking total *"share of customer."*

• **Industrial-age firms didn't have a clue who their customers were**. In a mass-production, mass-consumption era, they had no choice but to do mass advertising. The dubious rationale for advertising was that it let firms make more goods. The more they sold, they said, the more they could produce, lowering per-unit costs — and justifying ad spending. These firms blanketed radio air waves, TV screens, and printed pages with universal messages. Others bought zip-coded lists of apparently similar target segments of faceless customers, stuffing their mailboxes with junk mail.

Reaching everyone but no one in particular, they bought (at great cost!) *"share of market."*

• **Info-age merchants again will know each customer and their personal idiosyncracies**. They will keep that information in a computer data base and develop one-to-one lifelong relations with each customer. In the Info Age, the main function of advertising is not to expand product sales volume in a mass market (which no longer exists) but to highlight product value to individual customers throughout their lifetime.

New age merchants seek *"share of customer."*

We've come full circle. The *Global Village* is the marketing paradigm. Now, more than ever, *"the medium is the message."* Future success depends on understanding:
- "Demassified Media";
- Interactive "Tele-Media";
- "Mass-Customized" Advertising;
- Data-Base Marketing; and
- Personally Relevant Messages.

"Demassified" Media

Information technology reverses all processes. The mass media is rapidly "demassifying" as it scrambles to reach the splintered mass market. People simply want personally relevant information.

In print media, segmented publications sprout up as generic and national ones struggle to survive. The smart ones "glocalize." **Time-Warner** publishes a raft of special-interest magazines. Thanks to computerized typesetting, even its generic *Time* magazine publishes East and West Coast U.S. editions and, like the *Los Angeles Times*, seven versions in L.A. alone.

Thanks to computer dictionaries, stories run in the Canadian edition of *Time* even use British-English. They spell "color" as "colour" and note temperatures in °C not °F and distances in kilometers/meters/centimeters not miles/yards/feet/-inches.

Also, thanks to computers, magazines can reach individual subscribers through *personalized ink-jet printing* (personalizing an ad within the magazine) and through *selective binding* (tailoring page content to each reader). It's no wonder that newspapers are struggling.

To survive and prosper, *all* print media must become fully electronic. Many, including newspapers of course, already are available in data bases accessible by computer modem. Others *(as discussed below)* are converting themselves into TV channels. Meanwhile, newspapers must:

• **Increase individual reader utility.** People need more reasons to buy. Like **Gannett**'s *USA Today*, newspapers must be a more relevant, interactive partner in each reader's daily life. This ultimately can only be achieved through "mass-customized" full editions, not just fax summaries which, after all, will soon be as obsolete as newspaper clipping services. Moreover, the increasingly multiethnic population and burgeoning changes in social values will force editorial changes. Otherwise, the ethnic media will wipe out the traditional "WASP" press. Indeed, ethnic newspapers are already growing rapidly.

• **Change advertising structures.** In a fragmenting market, where anyone can publish a news-sheet on a PC, ad rates "per agate line" not only sound archaic, they are archaic. Market success isn't measured in column inches. Since media buyers relate to GRPs (gross rating points), papers must sell "share-of-market" space like radio and TV. Even then, in a "share-of-customer" world, GRPs will soon be as archaic as agate lines for display ads. Also, classified ads should be "pooled" electronically with those of other competing newspapers so buyers can one-stop shop by phone through a "Call Center."

• **Build subscriber data base.** In the end, to battle electronic ad delivery and personalized direct mail ads, a newspaper must build its own subscriber data base that plays on its strength as a household info-supplier. It can then provide advertisers with a narrowly defined market focus through guaranteed delivery of polybagged targeted ads on a specified day to specific customers. The days of mass circulation inserts and flyers are over. In short, papers should stop selling mass circulation figures and start selling specific audiences, right in their homes — household by household, reader by reader.

Many print media are converting to TV delivery. **Bell Atlantic**'s cable subsidiary, **Tele-Communications Incorporated (TCI)**, plans a dozen or more special interest channels through its *Vision Group* cable unit. It has agreed with **Hachette Filipacchi** to create an automotive channel based on its *Road & Track*, *Car & Driver*, and *Cycle World* magazines and another channel based on *Woman's Day* magazine. Similarly, **Meredith Corporation** is talking with **TCI** about developing programs based on several of its magazines, including *Better Homes & Gardens*.

As with mass print media, radio and TV "broadcasters" will continue losing audience to segmented "narrowcasters." In TV, apart from geographic localization, content demassification is already rampant. For example, *Diamond Vision* amuses fans at sporting events. *Health Club TV* is for fitness fanatics. *Mall Vision* is for shoppers in malls. *Concierge* has interactive reservation kiosks at airports. *Gourmet Channel* features food and eating programs. *Medical News* sells pharmaceuticals direct to doctors' offices. *MTV* entertains 10 million young people. *Channel One* goes right into the schools. The list goes on.

Radio and TV are also splintering along ethnic lines. There are now more than 2,000 Hispanic/Latino and African-American media outlets across America. *Bonjour Média* serves French-Canadian "snowbirds" who spend the winter in Florida. Japanese and Chinese channels serve major urban centers.

In short, the media world is going "glocal." Indeed, it's also going personally interactive.

Interactive Tele-Media

AT&T and **MCI** already offer "tele-media" services to marketers. Tele-media are interactive media used in advertising, marketing, and promotion via toll-free numbers. **Sprint**'s *FonMagic* adds toll-free 800/900-numbers to packages or ads, offering callers everything from free samples to contests and giveaways. **P&G** and **Lever Brothers** have tested tele-media where consumers hear a recorded message and, via interactive response, receive product info — or provide data useful for surveys and data banks. Other firms eying tele-media include **Coca-Cola**, **Pepsi-Cola**, **GM**, and **Kraft General Foods**.

NBC now has an 800-number *Viewer Service* that lets viewers get more info by mail about advertised products. It also publishes *NBC Preview*, a viewing guide mailed to viewers asking for it. Besides generating ad leads, the guide also produces a valuable data base. **News Corporation**'s *Fox* network also uses an 800-number that lets advertisers send coupons directly to viewers by the *Product Movers* and *Quad Marketing* coupon divisions of **News Corporation**.

KICU-TV (San Jose) is testing interactive ads and building a data base via a 24-hour info-line of news, weather, sports, business, flight info, TV programs, contests, community events, and infotainment. Ski conditions, tax tips, and pet-care may be added. Callers can win prizes in exchange for their name, address, phone number, and birth date, plus input on their travel, movie, and other service preferences. They also can instantly connect with advertisers such as **Great Western Bank** to open an account or **Bally's** to book a room. The station also teams up with advertisers to direct-market coupons, internally printing and direct-mailing them to potential buyers.

But those are simplistic systems. In full interactive TV (ITV), every viewer becomes a program producer. Programs must capture viewer imagination. Viewers of ITV don't passively watch an advertisement (or mute) it. Advertisers on ITV thus must do more than create long-form commercials or videos. They will sponsor customized news and sports reports and "involve" individual subscribers.

ITV ads can't push people to buy; they must pull prospects into the program so they can sell themselves on a product's value. For example, viewers will be able to click on any part of the ITV picture — say on *Baltimore Orioles'* second baseman Robby Alomar to get his career stats, or on his "golden" glove to get its brand name/price — and place an order.

Such interactive media engages buyers in a true 1:1 dialogue; it appeals to their specific interests. ITV is a two-way buyer-controlled info-appliance. By the late 1990s, of course, most of us will shop, bank, pay bills, order food, buy movie tickets, and organize TV or VCR programs with a *TeleCom Wallet*.

Meanwhile, in terms of TV shopping, electronic retailers must draw on these interactive lessons from the early TV shopping experience:

- Develop a cozy, intimate **rapport** with the viewing audience;
- Describe a **lifestyle** scene for the product in use (for example, "perfect for sailing");
- Sell products with features that are easy to **demonstrate** (such as cameras or vacuums);
- Present apparel in **primary colors** (complicated patterns look fuzzy);
- Make merchandise seem special, limited, and **unavailable elsewhere**;
- Viewers pay lots for shipping/handling, so goods must be seen as **bargains**;
- Hire celebrities to **glamorize** low-price items such as cosmetics.

People also buy via computer networks which, of course, can also be effective advertising channels.

American Airlines' *Sabre* system now carries ads aimed at travel agents. These are short, copy-only, paid ads which appear atop the screen when an agent signs on. Soon, ads will be placed in front of travelers. When an agent — or a customer at home — keys up flight info on a specific destination, the system will display an ad for a related hotel, car rental firm, or tourist attraction. This "global electronic travel agency" thus will sell "screen space" to advertisers. It achieves precise positioning, at the point of sale, reaching an audience with 100% efficiency.

On computer bulletin board service (BBS) networks such as **Internet**, however, traditional ad copy won't work. BBSs are a content-oriented, virtual "oral" community, where keyboards mediate the spoken word. Consumers can use search programs such as *Gopher* to navigate a universe of company or product info to locate and select exactly what they need in as much detail as they like.

Computer users appreciate quality, filtered information. To succeed, advertisers must "talk" with various subcultures and add value to passive messages. They must use content-based, interactive, community-oriented dialogue and be prepared to suitably engage in various forums. Messages should be couched within commentary on industry trends or latest public issues, perhaps in electronic newsletter format.

Better yet would be a *Usenet* special interest group for discussion of your products. Each group, on everything from amateur radio to gardening to travel, are both a form of a niche "focus group" and a self-organizing market segment.

These sophisticates do not buy simply because an ad tells them to. Customers expect to be fully informed about a product and its benefits to them personally. They want a dialogue that explains why they should buy. As McLuhan again saw, *"Propaganda ends where dialogue begins."*

What does that say about infomercials? Now used by direct marketers for one-stop selling, they are monologues not dialogues. To avoid being a passing fad, infomercials must be interactive and menu-driven. For example, an infomercial about luggage is too general for most viewers. It should be broken up into short segments: a brief intro about luggage followed by selectable options such as soft-sided, hard-sided, carry-on size, garment bags, packing tips, and so on. The use of virtual reality technology would really draw people into such presentations.

Clearly, ads which not only "inform" but "involve" the customer will gain most attention. Interactive media are perfect for reaching future consumers. They offer the chance to deliver a more personal ad message:

	Mass Media	**Interactive Media**
Audience	Consumer Segment	Single Consumer
Message	Assertive	Intriguing
Approach	Listen/Watch!	Wanna play?
Structure	Stereotypical	Personalized
Content	Expert Monologue	Friendly Dialogue
Intent	Emotive Brainwash	Educational
Goal	Recall/Purchase	Brand Relationship

Clearly, marketers who aim mass media ads *at* consumers are wasting their money. Future buyers will search out info-intensive ads of specific interest to them. Indeed, interactive TV (ITV) will lead to pay-per-view "info-ads."

Yes, customers *not* advertisers will pay for the ads!

Customers will use a *TeleCom Wallet* to tailor-make their own info-ads, picking out precisely what they need to know. They will zap any general ad which comes their way.

ITV thus will provide a more accurate measure of info-ad effectiveness: away from soft measures (awareness, attitude, and recall) to concrete changes in sales and market share.

Hence, measures of mass media "reach" are no longer relevant; personal "depth" is what counts. After all, there is no guarantee that ad recall leads to a purchase. For example, **IBM**'s brand name boasts a 98% awareness level, yet the firm has struggled to survive.

To paraphrase an old dictum: *"Tell/show me and I may remember; involve me and I'll learn."*

To succeed, ads will be both highly info-intensive and highly interactive — exactly the opposite of mass advertising *(see table, below)*.

INFO-INTENSIVE INTERACTIVE ADVERTISING		
	Level of Customer Interaction	
Level of Info-Intensive Content	**High**	**Low**
High	**Typical Products:** House, Car, Computer, Investment, Insurance, Vacation, Tailored Clothing **Suitable Media:** Interactive Media and Personal Sales	**Typical Products:** Appliance, Furniture, Concert Ticket, City Bus Tour, Cellphone, Caviar, Golf Clubs **Suitable Media:** Infomercials and Printed Brochures
Low	**Typical Products:** Prescribed Medicine, Two-line Telephone, Skin Cosmetics, Donation **Suitable Media:** Personalized Mail and Telemarketing	**Typical Products:** Newspaper/Magazine, Candy Bar, Movie, Golf Balls, Lipstick, Beer, Loaf of Bread **Suitable Media:** Traditional Print/Radio/TV Ads and Junk Mail

(Sources: Adapted from M. J. Cronin, *Doing Business on the Internet*, Van Nostrand Reinhold, New York 1994, and J. R. Rossiter and L. Percy, *Advertising and Promotion Management*, McGraw-Hill, New York 1987.)

"Mass-Customized" Advertising

Since glocal marketers can talk directly to individual buyers, traditional mass advertising will be less and less effective because 99% of customers simply don't fit the median or mean.

Positioning starts with individual customers and how they think about the firm and its product. Buyers, not advertisers, position products. Firms should focus less on differentiating *products* against competitive ones and focus more on differentiating each *customer* and their product/service needs.

Successful ads harmonize a consumer's senses to create intuitive bonds with a product. In the traditional mass market, effective ads created collective consumer bonding with a brand.

The info-intensity of the *Global Village* itself now creates a collective social consciousness. Info-intensity also reconfigures the producer-consumer value chain, weaving it into a networked "value web" of relationships. On the face of it, this should make mass advertising easier, cheaper, and more effective. Hence, all the hype about global advertising.

In the late 1980s, as discussed, too many big ad agencies peddled the benefits of global advertising and vastly oversold the idea. Grey Advertising, one of those that resisted the "global ad fad," advocated *Global Vision with Local Touch* — a maxim which is even more vital in the 1990s. Let's recall the assertion of **Coca-Cola**'s David Sanderson:

Few firms can do global advertising effectively. There are few brands where global standardization make sense.

You see, *Global Village* buyers are bombarded with 90,000 ad messages a year. The information *implosion* is splintering the market into smaller and smaller niches. The information *explosion* is increasing customer awareness but making them harder to reach. Moreover, mass advertising does not discriminate; but people do. As a result, consumers tune out and search for tailored info about their own specific buying needs.

A brand is like a tribal myth. In the "retribalized" *Global Village*, global ads must create a myth (that is, a personally relevant brand image). As with a person, a brand's overall image conveys intangible information to create a "virtual" personality. This entails conveying the kind of "halo" image that **Sony** has with innovation or **The Body Shop** has with ecology.

Hence, mass advertising must find a different future; it must become "glocal." Advertising must be orchestrated through a tiered hierarchy of ads which reinforce the "halo effect" of brands to deliver the product reality to individual customers.

Marketers must use a "mass-customized," precise (1:1) positioning matrix of:
- "Mass" Advertising (global/national/regional/local);

- "Cultural" Advertising (ethno/bio/psychographic);
- "Customized" Advertising (personal, one-to-one).

This matrix mirrors the "Glocal" Segmentation Strategy *(page 123, under "Mass-Customized Product")*, as follows:

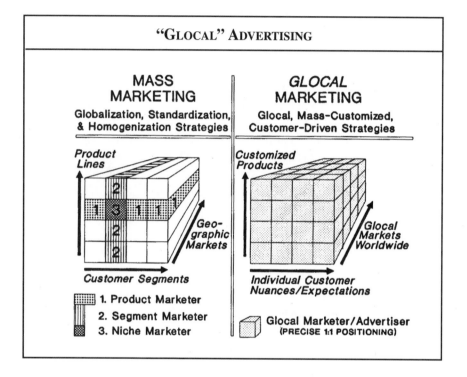

"Mass" Advertising

The new purpose of mass advertising is to use fewer, more effective ads to create brand "personality" at the global, national, regional, and local levels, using relevant tie-ins over "broadcast" and "narrowcast" media.

Yet most brands are still marketed with one dull strategy and with unpositioned, unexciting execution. Ads only work globally (or nationally) if they make sense locally — and if they jive with each consumer's personal values and beliefs.

Successful glocal ads have a consistent universal theme that "travels" and are executed so that local cultural barriers do not thwart them. Such ads should be highly visual, feature the brand name, and convey the overall theme with transcultural and personally relevant "myth" symbols.

Some companies simply position themselves as "glocal." For example, **Swiss Bank Corporation**'s ad slogan is:

The key to intelligent investing: local market presence and global network.

In 1994, Japan's **Sanwa Bank** began using an ad with a satellite image of planet Earth and the following "glocal" ad copy:

SANWA BANK INTRODUCES *GLOCAL BANKING.*
There is no Alternative.

Most banks follow one of two courses: global banking or local banking. But global banking often loses sight of local conditions, local needs. And local banking lacks the reach and the perspective to serve your needs around the world. Which is why the introduction of *glocal banking* is important news. Sanwa provides a full range of financial services tailored to meet *local* needs in every city where we do business. And, beyond that, access to Sanwa's *global* network; a formidable resource only a bank that ranks among the four largest in the world could provide. Local needs; global strength.

So see Sanwa Bank.
See what a difference *glocal banking* can make.

"Glocal" or not, global ads must be supported with local ads. Mahatma Gandhi said that, to get noticed, you shouldn't follow the crowd but stand on your head — do something different.

To get attention — to stand out in crowded media — ads must mirror local market taste and culture. To keep attention, you must use a consistent global image and a relevant local message. Local ad agencies thus will be increasingly important, tailoring campaigns to local market nuances while maintaining global brand integrity.

Coca-Cola, for instance, does use a global pool of ads for use in various markets. But it makes local adaptations, and not just for language. In 1991, it created a global campaign for 50 countries but made 35 versions. In effect, they used the same ad but each adaptation featured something specific to a particular market or group of consumers.

In 1992, **Coca-Cola** made a variety of ads for state-specific campaigns in America. With a theme *Wisconsin Proud*, a humorous **Coke** truck driver roamed the state to learn why folks lived there. The ads featured local traditions such as fishing, music, and favorite foods. Other themes included *Texas: Home of the Real Thing*, and *Minnesota: We've got it all.*

Coca-Cola also went "glocal" in Canada, creating a pool of 26 TV commercials, each designed for a specific customer group. Under a theme *"Always Coke,"* the ads varied in style, theme, and length. **Coke (Canada)** president Tony Eames says the spots were based on **Coke**'s "four pillars" of:

- always there (responding anyplace/anytime);
- always new (reinterpreted for each generation);
- always real (reflecting values of family, friends, fun);
- always you (relevant to each consumer personally).

Clearly, no matter how common the product or well-known the brand — nor how large the company — there is no choice but to "glocalize" the entire positioning effort.

Even camera film cannot be positioned in a standard fashion. **Kodak**, like **Coca-Cola**, has a global pool of ads for different markets, with local agencies creating specific tactical efforts and campaign messages. **Corel** positions its *CorelDRAW* computer software differently in 120 magazines in 60 countries. **Harlequin** commissions romances for more than 100 markets in more than 20 languages. **Reader's Digest** puts out 39 different editions in 17 languages. **Canon** positions cameras for replacement buyers in Japan, upscale first-time buyers in the U.S., and technically sophisticated buyers in Germany.

Ford has a three-tier U.S. strategy, "glocalizing" ads through 63 local dealer groups. **McDonald's** also has an "inverted pyramid," explained by local market manager Bob Kitterman:

National advertising seeds programs down through 37 regions and 180 co-op districts. At the local store level, that translates into empowerment to drive local sales.

Nike introduced a local marketing program in 1992, and **Reebok** tried regional marketing in 1994, empowering local offices to design and execute field marketing programs, including radio campaigns. **Paramount Pictures** also shifted to local advertising in 1993. Observes Arthur Cohen, head of global marketing:

For every dollar we put up, we can generate 15-20 times that dollar in measured media promotional support via the local ad agency network.

Radio is one of the best media to reach local buyers. Local by its very nature, radio is deeply involved with listeners and knows what's happening locally. And smart firms are really making sure their scarce ad dollars are where they need them to be to sell their product. Monthly tracking of ad spending by the Radio Advertising Bureau shows that the use of local radio ads is growing by 75%. Firms active in radio are brewers, telcos, travel companies, and car makers. Sam Michaelson, VP of **Saatchi & Saatchi** (the "global ad" advocate), admits:

Advertisers are refocusing and going to the consumer roots — the local level.

Gerber also ties into local communities through local media and retailers.

Marketing manager Ian Lum-You credits three elements for the successful launch of *Graduates*: radio ads, precise positioning, and local retailer support *(see box)*.

GERBER'S LOCAL AD STRATEGY

Gerber's local market programs generally tend to run for 4-6 weeks in each market and provide each participating retailer with one week of co-op radio advertising.

• Radio Advertising
Local ads create local identity for national brands, thus strengthening brand equity. Radio is the most effective vehicle, offering flexibility in targeting groups such as teens, working women, or sports fans. A good radio station knows the hot buttons of its market.

Note: Radio is the "Baby Boomer" companion: clock radios wake them; car radios ease daily commutes and weekend drives; radio music soothes office work and power lunches; and radios enliven outdoor BBQs, beach parties, and picnics.

• Local Retailer Support
Retailer support is critical to local market success. Participating retailers are provided with local radio advertising support to promote their stores along with **Gerber**'s products. This comes in the form of a 30-second commercial married to a 30-second brand or product promo to form a "30/30" co-op radio spot. These 30-second commercials are provided "free" to local retailers in exchange for in-store merchandising such as feature pricing or display.

• Precisely Positioned Promotions
Promotions must be customer-focused to create market pull. On-air promotions may range from mail-in contests for trips and merchandise to instant-win programs where consumers are rewarded with prizes for purchasing a product or for participating in an on-air contest. Promos need to have strong appeal to the target group in their local community. They should tie into local events or charity drives and use local retailer tie-ins as part of the prize package.

(Source: Gerber Canada published documents)

"Cultural" Advertising

The second part of "Mass-Customized" advertising is "Cultural" advertising, which we'll examine under two headings:
- Ethnic Advertising; and
- Generational Advertising.

Ethnic Advertising

By now you'll agree that an acute sensitivity to cultural nuance is of growing importance in North America — as John Ball, ethnic marketing manager of **Quaker Oats** observes:

As we learn about ethnic marketing, we find traditional marketing programs are less effective than targeted ones.

Fortunately, although everything in the multicultural "Salad Bowl" is mixed up, you can easily spot the cucumber, mushroom, olive, onion, radish, and tomato. Indeed, rather than becoming tougher as immigrants flood in, culture-sensitive marketing becomes easier.

Of course, a firm that already enjoys brand equity in the immigrants' home countries has a market edge when those people come here. And loyal immigrant customers will transfer brand equity back to their home markets, helping the firm expand globally.

Word of mouth plays a large role among immigrants, so brand prestige and popularity back home are strong motivators. But a firm must take account of how familiar are its brands and whether they're even sold under the same names back home. If so, since most immigrants settle in communities of their own culture, brand awareness among existing community members has much influence on newcomers.

Immigrant or not, each ethnic culture must be appealed to differently. Entire books have been written on how to reach various ethnic groups. By way of *brief* example — and only for African-, Hispanic/Latino-, Asian-, and Arab-Americans — here are some points to ponder.

• African-Americans

Sprinkling black faces in ads conceived for a white audience isn't nearly enough. African-Americans are very sensitive to social values presented in ads. Black experience is rooted in the struggle for respect, belonging, and achievement in what is still a white-dominated culture. Inserting a few black people into commercials, for products that otherwise lack black cultural appeal, merely adds insult to injury.

Rather, ads which wish to appeal to African-Americans must use African-Americans as the central characters. **USAir**, for example, uses an ad which features a black woman executive on her way to give an important speech. Patricia Dewey, senior ad director argues:

A world-class airline should project American diversity. We'll get more minority revenue and earn more loyalty generally because that's what people expect to see.

• Hispanics/Latinos

The Hispanic/Latino group is not homogenous. The Cubans of Florida differ from New York's Puerto Ricans or the Mexicans and Central Americans in the Southwest. So ads that work well in Miami or New York won't do so well in San Antonio. Hispanics/Latinos who think of themselves as assimilated also differ from those who are not. Those who mostly speak English also differ from those who mostly speak Spanish. So, while ad copy written in informal spoken Spanish works best, you must be careful *(see boxes on following pages)*.

Although colorful, most Hispanics/Latinos do not identify with materialistic displays of success, but do see themselves as upbeat and lively and want to be portrayed as such. Music will help achieve this, but color must be used carefully. Purple, for example, is linked with death in most Spanish cultures, but yellow flowers mean death to Mexicans. Family is also important, and Latino women have traditional ambitions. Hispanics also vehemently reject ads that are dubbed onto "white" ads or ones that do not reflect their values and lifestyle.

Filipino immigrants also should be seen as part of this group. The Philippines is a former Spanish colony. So, while Filipinos are well educated and fluent in English and sometimes Spanish, at home they speak their native Tagalog. Like Hispanics/Latinos, they also follow strong family values.

• Asian-Americans

Southeast Asians are the fastest growing segment of many markets. A sophisticated group, they also are better-educated than most African-Americans, Hispanics, or whites. They like lots of information, and brands should be portrayed for their "quality" rather than as ones used by "Orientals."

Among various values, most southeast Asian people want a "harmonious" relationship, that is, having security, a sense of belonging, and warm relations with others. Since their culture is primarily based on a state of coexistence, their top five wishes in life are for health, security, happiness, freedom, and wealth — so ads should reflect those Confucian values.

• Arab-Americans and Muslims

Islam is a way of life and Muslims from various parts of the world should not really be lumped together. In general, however, the family is the key social unit. For example, airlines who are unable to seat husband and wife together will face the wrath of an indignant and insistent husband. Father is the supreme decision-maker, and individual buying decisions are seldom made without significant family input. And, despite the image of rich Arabian sheiks, Muslims in general value making friends more than making money.

The traditional Arabian bazaar (*souk*) is a popular place for social interaction where people improve their haggling skills. This carries over into attitudes about shopping: supermarkets are not time-savers but an excuse to go out and shop frequently. Muslim consumers also do not easily accept new products and feel more comfortable with proven brands.

Simply stated, to achieve top-of-mind awareness with *all* ethnic groups, you must use *their* media and speak *their* "language." *Global Village* buyers respond best to ads when their language is culture-sensitive (*see boxes below and overleaf*).

A perfect way to reflect the new America is a recent TV advertisement by **Schick**. Wanting to be *"truer to the market and to people's perception that they live in a multicultural world,"* **Schick** transformed the "all-American guy." Its

---

CULTURE-SENSITIVE ADVERTISING
— Language —

• **Sprint** uses 18 languages in ads, marketing, and PR efforts for its global long-distance telephone calling plan.

• **P&G** promotes *Tide*, *Downy*, *Comet*, and *Dawn* in 18 major U.S. markets in English and Spanish. It also targets African-Americans with *Crest*, *Tide*, *Downy* — and *Cover Girl* cosmetics.

• **Unilever** renamed its *Snuggle* fabric softener as *FaFa* in Japan, *Coccolino* in Italy, and other cuddly sounding names elsewhere.

• **Kraft General Food**'s *Tang* failed in Germany because it means "seaweed." Renamed *Seefrisch* ("see-fresh"), it was a big success.

• **PepsiCo**'s slogan, *"Come alive with the Pepsi generation,"* was mistranslated in Taiwan as "Pepsi brings ancestors back to life."

• **Coca-Cola** first launched *Coke* in China with a name meaning "bite the wax tadpole." When changed to "happiness in the mouth," sales bubbled. **Coke**'s slogan *"It's the real thing"* has an off-color Spanish meaning and had to be changed.

• **North American Life**'s name literally translates into Chinese as *Bo Mei* which also could mean "not fulfilling." So the insurance company used *Ga Mei* which means "Canada and America Life" and "added value."

• **Chevrolet**'s *Nova* brand name translates into *no va*, meaning "it doesn't go"! **Ford**'s *Pinto* meant "a small male appendage."

TV ads use a "morphing" effect to seamlessly blend several faces — Caucasian, Asian, Hispanic, and African-American — dissolving each into the other in a shaving mirror.

Image, as well as the use of colors and shapes, can be very important, whether advertising in multicultural North America or in the world at large *(see box, below)*.

CULTURE-SENSITIVE ADVERTISING
— Numbers —

Brand names with numbers in them are perceived differently:
• **Large numbers** (*Boeing 747*) imply technical quality, greater performance/complexity, sophistication, and precision.
• **Sequential numbers** (*Word Perfect 5.1 ... 6.0*) imply a more recent product in a series.
• **Low numbers** (*3M* or *Lotus 1-2-3*) imply exclusivity.
• **Rhyming numbers** (*7-Eleven*) catch attention and aid recall.
• **Repeated digits** (*Boeing 777*) are easier to remember.
• **Written script** (*Saks 5th Avenue*) evokes wealth/elegance.
• **Mixed letters/numbers** (*Mazda RX-7* or *Oral B-40*) imply technical sophistication.

To the Chinese, some numbers have lucky connotations:
• **Alpha Romeo** renamed its model *164* the *168* in Hong Kong. The sound of "164" in Cantonese (the south China dialect) meant "all the way to death," while "168" sounds like "all the way to prosperity." Sales promptly took off.
• **Royal Bank of Canada** attributes the success of a financial hotline for Chinese customers to the liberal use of 3s and 8s which, to Chinese, indicate liveliness and prosperity.

CULTURE-SENSITIVE ADVERTISING
— Color, Shape, Image —

• **Color**

In Confucian cultures such as Chinese or Japanese, white is the color of mourning. Red and gold represent prosperity. The colors of the 190+ national flags, found in any atlas, basically reveal the pet colors and symbols of most cultures. Even then, there are 1,000 cultures. So ethnic groups respond to yet different symbols.

• **Shape**

Most cultures have a different concept of space and size than we do. For instance, since storage space is scarce in Japanese homes, **P&G**'s Japanese ads for *Tide* stress compact packaging.

• **Image**

P&G culturally adapted its *Camay* soap ads in Venezuela to show a beautiful woman lathering herself in the bath, with a man also seen in the bathroom. In Italy and France, only the man's hand was seen. In Japan, he waited discretely outside. Even then, this image was a cultural *faux pas* because Japanese lather-up *before* getting in the bath. They also thought it rude to show a lady bathing.

• **"Universal" Image**

Sometimes a universal image can "travel" across cultures. **Fendi** thus conveys the idea of classic elegance for its wristwatch with a universally understood image of classical Rome. **Jaeger** uses a richly appointed room and impeccably groomed model to convey an unmistakable aristocratic aura for its men's clothing.

• **Local Image**

A recent survey of 120 European commercials found British consumers indignant toward a French ad where the man of the house poured tea. Germans were annoyed by Italian women swilling beer while men drank it alone. A British-made ad for *Buitoni* pasta, using shots of Rome, scored higher in Britain than the Italian-made version, while a standardized Pan-European message scored lowest. The message: exploit a product's genuine cultural roots to the fullest extent.

Generational Advertising

Care must also be used in appealing to our "Generations of 2004." Again, entire books discuss how to reach various age groups, but here are a few pointers. Because they're the *future* consumers, I'll say a tad more about the later generations.

• "By-the-Book" Angry Reactives (born 1911-28)

Elderly people stop buying products where ads stereotype them by age. They prefer the terms "mature" (28%) or "senior" (24%) instead of "old" or "elderly." Brought up by parents raised in Victorian times, ads should be clear-cut and orderly and appeal to solid old-fashioned values. Anything risqué is totally taboo.

• "By-the-Clock" Repressed Conformists (born 1929-45)

You should also refer to this group as "mature" or "senior." These folks "won" WWII and the Cold War so treat them with the respect they expect. Present lots of detail in an orderly fashion. Use the "right stuff" to appeal to loyalist values of hard work and "doing the right thing," and you'll be on the right track. Just imagine you're advertising to George Bush.

• "Baby Boom" Overconfident Idealists (born 1946-64)

For most of this group, the crass commercialism of the 1980s has given way to the typical middle-aging concerns of health and financial security. Here your focus should be lifestyle enhancement and appeals to lofty ideals such as saving the planet. A "green" and socially responsible image is essential.

They'll also pay a lot of attention to information on product packages and in brochures and advertisements. Many of these people think they "know it all," so don't shortchange them here. And don't try to "snow" them; bogus claims will boomerang. Extra product features will have less appeal than the genuine benefits a product will have for them personally and for the planet in general.

Seeking products that will see them through at least to retirement, they'll also be concerned about reliability and durability. Blue-chip brand names will be back in vogue.

• "Generation X" Angry Reactives (born 1965-82)

While technical wizardry will be expected by this group, images of the "Baby Boomer" world will not. They dismiss suburban housing developments as *"blockish, senseless, enormous brick houses, one inch apart and three feet from a highway."* Who can disagree? Suffering from what they call *"architectural indigestion,"* they also reject shopping malls (where they had to spend far too much of their youth).

You cannot pigeonhole them. In his book *Generation X*, Douglas Coupland proclaims: *"I am not a target market!"*

What to do? Being media sophisticates, "Generation Xers" reject slick packaging and distrust hype and "spin" wherever they see it. To them, ads are pop culture. Only clever images, humor, and irreverence in *"ads which admit that they are ads"* are well-received.

Intolerant of and wanting to solve various social ills, they appreciate issue-oriented ads which discuss AIDS, abortion, drugs, crime, racial or other forms of discrimination, and the environment (90% of this group is "green"). Not surprisingly, **Benetton**'s controversial "issues" ads are "cool" with this group, as is **Schick**'s racial "morphing" ad *(see pages 153-155).*

• "Real-Time" Repressed Conformists (born 1983-2000)

This colorful *Global Village* generation takes technical sophistication and transcultural and trans-gender values as the norm. Growing up on the info superhighway, they expect to spend their entire lives there — "learning a living." It *is* their world. These information hunters and gatherers will not just reject ads targeted at them, they simply won't notice them. Rather they will custom-make (and pay for) their own ads. And that brings us to the real future of advertising.

"Customized" Advertising

Of course, simply using a geographic/ethnic/generational advertising blend still doesn't "reach" consumers personally. It isn't "deep" enough!

Indeed, most companies don't have a clue who their customers are. Do *you* know the name, address, phone number, and bio-data of each of *your* company's clients?

In trying to find out, firms waste pots of money on generic market research that still leaves them in the dark about their customers. Then they waste zillions on useless mass promo and ad campaigns trying to reach faceless, nameless clients.

In 1992, for example, **Pepsi-Cola** sent out 40 million cases of soft drinks along with *Gotta Have It Cards* which offered discounts on a range of products. (A "six-pack" of *Diet Pepsi* was left on my doorstep, even though I'm a loyal *Coke Classic* sipper and nobody else in my household likes *Pepsi* either.) The recipients didn't have to become "members" and couldn't collect points on any subsequent purchases. In sum, no data base of loyal customers was created and **Pepsi-Cola** still didn't know who its customers were. Such blind, mass promotion achieves zero positioning.

Because individual customer loyalty is key to future success in a splintered market, companies must develop a one-to-one approach using an in-house data base of *precise*, fully detailed info on *each* customer.

Data-Base Marketing

Data-Base Marketing (DBM) uses *mass* storage technology to achieve *individual* marketing. Rather than a generic *demo*graphic data base, it keeps specific *bio-*

graphic files. These files include "stage-of-life" events such as a job change, marriage, new baby, birthday, graduation, or retirement — each tracked over time.

DBM thus lets you coordinate precise, personal communication with each customer. It brings personal marketing to the high-tech age.

In detail, a bio-data base lets you:
- Track individual customer purchases, attitudes, wants, needs, and desires;
- Initiate local matrix mailings based on a complete customer biographic-info and transaction history;
- Select a target, segment a file, deliver a personal marketing message, and get a response in seconds;
- Target segments *within* the individual, not segments *of* individuals (e.g., **Red Lobster** is *"for the sea food lover in you,"* not for people who love sea food);
- Chart local market share and forecast local demand;
- Design, develop, and test products with high assurance;
- Deliver ads to each household, "knocking" on all the right doors (not every door) in the neighborhood.

Such personal marketing is about what customers want (not what the company needs). It's driven by value-based customer-controlled interaction. **MCI**, for example, cleverly gathers competitive info while rewarding loyal customers under its *Friends & Family* program. People get discounts when they phone others in their "calling circle" who are also **MCI** customers. So they willingly give the names and phone numbers of friends and family to **MCI** which then tries to persuade them also to use the service.

Modern firms thus use *cold* computers to build *warm* bonds with customers. They "knock" on the right doors with a data base *(see box, opposite)*. As observed by Robert Smith, senior VP of **RJR Nabisco**:

The mass market has shattered into hundreds of mini-markets. To address those markets, the technology and marketing sides of business must share information and work together as never before.

To get to know customers by name, some firms use membership clubs to create a data base of loyal customers *(see box on page 160)*. These firms know exactly who their customers are.

Examples of Data Base Marketing (DBM)

• **Quaker Oats** has spent $20 million to create a DBM system. Promotion director, Dan Strunk, asserts:

Household marketing is going to be the only way a consumer packaged goods company will compete in the future.

• **Kraft General Foods** has built a relational data base of 25 million brand-user households in the U.S. alone. It thus communicates directly with various segments, rolling out uniquely tailored products simultaneously in what it calls "locally dispersed" markets.

• **Pizza Hut** spent $20 million to create electronic profiles of some 9 million people who get pizza deliveries. It sends new customers welcoming greetings and rewards moderate users with new menu items.

• **Sears** has a data base of 30 million households. When a customer charges a purchase, the store knows what was bought. It groups people into household types that share common traits. It can then communicate personally with loyal and prospective customers.

• **Kimberly Clark**, the maker of *Huggies* diapers, has set up a DBM of the names of expectant mothers.

• **Brady's**, a men's clothing store, uses *Segment-of-One Marketing* to track each client's buying preferences.

• **Labatt** has a data base of 65,000 people that is brand-specific but can be cross-referenced. It claims that specialty brands serving smaller markets will benefit by direct marketing.

• **Auto Source**, the U.S. division of **Canadian Tire**, uses a data base to communicate with customers every six weeks on car maintenance, recalls, and various service specials.

Personally Relevant Messages

Finally, market presentation must also be "issues-relevant" to be customer-relevant.

Future consumers will make purchases on the basis of a firm's role in society: how it treats employees, shareholders, and local neighborhoods, and the way it addresses the various community issues identified earlier. Consumers will reward companies which work hard to address these issues.

MEMBERSHIP CLUB DATA BASES

- **Shiseido**, the Japanese cosmetics giant, has built a 10-million-strong *Shiseido Club*. Members get a *Shiseido Visa* card, discounts at hotels, theaters, and retailers, and earn "frequent buyer" points on purchases. **Shiseido** also puts out a magazine, given free to customers by the company's own stores and other retailers.
- **Nintendo** is building a data base via its 5-million-strong *Nintendo Fun Club*. Customer loyalty is so high that the Club dropped its free newsletter and launched a $15/year magazine, *Nintendo Power*. This promptly got 2 million readers — the most successful magazine launch in world history.
- **AT&T** publishes *Information On Call* magazine, containing product offers and service information from paid advertisers such as **Ford**, **United Airlines**, **Club Med,** and **Bon Appetit**. Consumers select info they want to receive (such as automotive, travel, cooking, or health) *via* a one-page questionnaire that gives **AT&T** valuable info for its data base.
- **P&G** has launched *Straight Scoop* club for female teenagers. They get a newsletter plus coupons and samples of eight products: *Crest, Oil of Olay, Vidal Sassoon, Secret, Always, Ban de Soleil, Clearasil,* and *Navy*. The company is also testing a quarterly magazine mailed to frequent shoppers of key supermarket chains.
- **Federal Express** woos executive assistants and receptionists (the people who usually decide who to use for overnight delivery) with *Via FedEx*, a free quarterly magazine with more than 1 million readers.
- **Nike** publishes a *Women's Resource Book* to better reach women and is building a data base of female customers.

Picking up on 1994's anticrime wave, for example, **Dallas Cowboys** (in conjunction with **Children's Medical Center** and the **Dallas Police**) gave free tickets to people who turned in guns.

A powerful 30-second public service TV commercial reenacted a teen's shooting and featured warnings from **Cowboys** defensive lineman Tony Casillas. The ad's clever tag line was:

"Real Cowboys Don't Carry Guns."

Wal-Mart no longer sells handguns for a simple reason:

"The mood of the country is changing, and customers say they would prefer not to shop where handguns are sold."

Other firms joined in the anticrime crusade. A stunningly successful *"Toys-for-Guns"* exchange in New York attracted support from **Toys "R" Us**, **Foot Locker**, and **Reebok** who gave $100 gift certificates in exchange for turned-in weapons. For **Reebok**, it was a natural extension of its $2 million program which offers after-school activities to keep youths off street corners and out of trouble.

Retailers also are venturing back into the inner cities many abandoned in the 1960s. **Vons** is spending $100 million to build stores in inner-city neighborhoods. **Ben & Jerry's** waived its usual $25,000 franchise fee and donated an ice-cream store in New York's Harlem district to local businessman Joe Holland. Most profits go to *HARKhomes*, Holland's program for homeless men. The store provides training and jobs for the residents, and its menu has a *Harlem Blues-berry* flavor. **The Body Shop** also has a bustling store in Harlem. Staffed entirely by residents, half the profits go to the community. The other half funds similar new stores elsewhere, with the next planned for the South Central district of Los Angeles.

The biggest issue, of course, is the "green" issue, and, as we've seen, many firms are responding to new consumer expectations on ecology.

Even **Business Week** magazine, appealing to the "green" mindset of new subscribers, arranges for the American Forestry Association to plant a tree in their name in one of America's Heritage Forests through the AFA's *Global ReLeaf Program*.

The tear-out subscription card (printed on recycled paper) somewhat breathlessly proclaims:

"Finally. An offer worth the paper it's printed on."

Has the media finally got the new message?

I hope *this* book (entirely made of recycled materials) is worth both the paper it's printed on and your time in reading it.

The Bottom Line:

Marketing is clearly shifting focus: from vast amounts of mass-market info to "mass-customized" info at the individual customer level. Using data in interactive files, marketers can establish the type of "personal" relationships shopkeepers once had with customers. Instead of single-mindedly chasing new customers, managers can focus on "aftermarketing" to retain existing customers through personalized messages.

Cynics say that 50% of advertising spending is wasted, but we don't know which 50%. Now we do. If campaigns don't jive with individual customer needs, *all* ad spending is wasted!

Maybe Will Rogers was right when he said: *"Let advertisers spend the same amount of money improving their product as they do advertising it, and they wouldn't have to advertise it."*

One thing's for sure, the best payoff comes from glocal campaign synergy, "glocalized" ads, and precise (1:1) positioning. Ad budgets must shift to support glocal efforts — to the long-term building of brand equity and "share of customer." Advertising must become customer-driven not product-driven.

How much market research and advertising money are *you* wasting? Shouldn't *you* create a glocal marketing mix which precisely matches *your* future consumer needs?

Checklist for "Glocal" Marketers

It's time to move beyond the mass-marketing myths of the Industrial Age; time to "glocalize" and "mass-customize" your marketing mix and create the new 4-Ps of the Information Age:

"Mass-Customized" Product/Service
✓ People are more unique than products, so differentiate customers not products.
✓ There are no universal products; remember, *"only milk should be homogenized."*
✓ Adapt all products to cultural nuance (ethnic and milieu) and resultant individual mindset and product usage.
✓ Target "glocally," with "mass-customized" products and services.
✓ Focus on "share of customer" to build "share of market."
✓ Replace "Product Managers" with "Customer Managers."
✓ Make all products "green" *and* recyclable.

AnyTime + AnyPlace Delivery/Access
✓ Use a whole-channel *AnyTime/AnyPlace* approach.
✓ Focus on electronic channels (ETKs, phones, PCs); they're easier/cheaper for the futuristic consumer.
✓ Try to deliver products/services direct to the client's home or place of business, electronically or person-to-person.
✓ However, avoid being intrusive/abusive. Telemarketing should be used only for customers who want it.
✓ Use satellites for site selection and tailor each outlet and its product offerings to its neighborhood or customer type.
✓ Set up a "Point of Recycle" (POR) for products.

Total Value Price
✓ "Glocalize" all prices.
✓ Eliminate discounts, incentives, promotions: they devalue brand equity.
✓ Compete against discounters with service, quality, convenience, and custom-tailored local neighborhood offerings.

✓ Adopt "no-dicker" every day low pricing (EDLP) to restore brand equity and boost profit margins.

✓ Stress product "benefits" and hike prices to "total" value levels.

✓ Use "purchase perks" to value-enhance the entire customer experience and build brand equity.

✓ Eliminate paper coupons or electrify and personalize them; even then, use them only for product introductions or to reward genuine brand loyalty.

Precise (1:1) Positioning

✓ Forget about "promotion" (it devalues brand equity) and start "precise one-to-one positioning" of product benefits.

✓ Stop buying generic market research. Invest in your own unique Data-Base Marketing (DBM) capability, perhaps with a free membership club publication.

✓ Forget the "global ad fad." Invariably, you must adapt all ads to local conditions and individual cultural values.

✓ Manage media positioning through a tiered hierarchy of "mass-customized advertising" that is:
> • mass (global/national/regional/local);
> • cultural (ethno/bio/psychographic);
> • customized (personal, one-to-one).

✓ Use demassified "glocal" media at each level, that is from mass global media, down through local media, to personalized household-by-household, person-by-person media.

✓ Stop the sales and advertising hype; make "info-ads" (that does *not* mean infomercials) which educate people about the product, and it will sell itself.

✓ Don't advertise *at* customers; engage them in an interactive, info-intensive, educational dialogue.

✓ Be sensitive to cultural nuances in "info-ad" copy, colors, shapes, and images — both in multicultural North America and across the world.

✓ Position the company as being a community and personally relevant offerer through "issues-oriented" communications. Above all, be "green" in all you do and make sure your customers know you are environmentally proactive.

IT'S TIME TO
REMAKE YOUR COMPANY

*Only the supremely wise
and abysmally ignorant
do not change.*

Confucius

The Chinese have a unique sense of the crisis of change. Their word for "crisis" combines two characters which, used separately, mean "danger" and "hidden opportunity."

Though change may be risky, it holds the promise of new opportunities. As John Dewey said, *"To those fully alive, the future is not ominous but a promise; it surrounds the present like a halo."*

It's time to grasp that promise.

Candidly, to ignore, shrink from, or dismiss the big Info Age shift to mass-customized glocal marketing is to commit corporate suicide and miss the biggest business bonanza in history.

To make superficial corporate changes or merely tinker with your organizational structure, its culture, or your marketing mix will achieve nothing. You need dramatic change; you need to remake your company in the image of the future consumer.

You see, the anomalous *Global Village* is the new paradigm of world affairs, business, and our personal lives. Exploiting that "glocal" anomaly through the Glocal Marketing Model is the key to business success in the Information Age.

Of course, the "Checklists" I have provided to help you refocus are generic. It is beyond the scope of this short book to provide mass-customized implications for each industry or type of business.

If you work through the Five-Step Glocal Marketing Model, however, and learn from the many industry/company-specific examples provided, you can draw implications unique to your own business and its product or service offerings.

I challenge you to do so — and dare you to dream of the success that can be yours in the new and exciting glocal marketing era.

If your company can tap the "virtual reality" of the glocal market, I guarantee that you will respond better and faster to future consumer needs, and outperform all competitors.

Who says you can't win 'em all?

May the glocal forces be with you!

Acknowledgments

SHAPED BY "GLOCAL" MINDS

In the Information Age, all authors owe so much to the explosion of knowledge flowing from other writers and thinkers.

This book is shaped by three pioneer "glocal" minds: media-mystic Marshall McLuhan; info-icon Yoneji Masuda; and glocal-guru Akio Morita of Sony Corp. I'm also indebted to the insights of the other authors cited in the Bibliography.

I also appreciate the encouragement and support of Ross Roberts (Ford), John Cranor and Dennis Frezzo (Pepsi/KFC), Phil Kotler (Northwestern University), Chuck DeRidder (U.S. Forest Service), and others too numerous to mention. But they know who they are.

Participant input at a string of speeches, seminars, and executive briefings helped inestimably in unearthing valuable case material. None of this was possible without the efforts of my lecture agency, the Leigh Bureau. Thanks go to Bill Leigh, Larry Leson, Tom Neilssen, Danny Stern, Ron Szymanski, Les Tuerk, Fern Webber, and their ever-supportive colleagues.

Special thanks go to Ron Szymanski for reading several drafts of the manuscript. Always insightful and constructive, he challenged me to rework the ideas until they flowed together. His unstinting enthusiasm for the project has been priceless.

I also appreciate the energetic support of Jim Williamson and Nick Pitt at Warwick Publishing.

Last, but not least, my deep appreciation to my best friend, intellectual partner, and loving wife, Tammie Tan, for her ever-present support and creative input as the manuscript developed.

Thank you all!

Frank Feather

About the Author

He's been called *"a walking encyclopedia on the future."* Frank Feather, the world's leading business futurist, is founder and president of Glocal Marketing Inc., and editor of the *Future Consumer Newsletter*.

Having coined the term *Thinking Globally, Acting Locally* in 1979, this ever-more valid maxim now underpins his *Glocal Marketing* concept for the late 1990s and beyond.

A former bank strategic planner, Frank has consulted to Ciba-Geigy, Exxon, Ford, Hewlett-Packard, IBM, ICI, KFC, Nissan, Northern Telecom, Nynex, Pitney-Bowes, Shell, and Volkswagen. He also advises the U.N., the IMF/World Bank, the governments of Mexico and Canada, and has consulted to China on economic and market reforms since 1984.

Also much sought-after on the lecture circuit, his recent audiences include education and health professionals, plus executives in the auto, banking, chemical, computer, energy, food, grocery, pharmaceutical, and telecom sectors.

An Executive Member of American Marketing Association (AMA) and a Fellow of the World Association for Social Psychiatry, he is a member of the World Future Society and also cofounded the Global Futures Network.

Frank's previous book, *G-FORCES: The 35 Global Forces Restructuring Our Future*, proved popular in America, Canada, and Japan. Others include *Optimistic Outlooks*; *THROUGH THE EIGHTIES: Thinking Globally, Acting Locally*; and *Canada's BEST CAREERS Guide*.

His next book, coauthored with his Chinese-born wife Tammie Tan, is *CHINA VISION: Region- and Sector-Specific Business and Personal Investment Strategies for the World's Hottest Market.*

Bibliography

Ames,B.C. & Hlavacek,J.D. *Market-Driven Management* (Homewood: Irwin, 1989).

Armstrong,F.A. *Shut Down the Home Office* (NY: Fine, 1991).

Badaracco,J.L. *The Knowledge Link* (Cambridge: Harvard U.Press, 1991).

Barabba,V.P. & Zaltman,G. *Hearing Market Voice* (Cambridge: Harvard UP, 1991).

Block,P. *The Empowered Manager* (San Francisco: Jossey-Bass, 1987).

Brand,S. *The Media Lab* (NY: Penguin, 1988)

Buzzell,R.D. *Marketing in an Electronic Age* (Cambridge: Harvard U.Press, 1985).

Cronin,M. *Doing Business on the Internet* (NY: Van Nostrand Reinhold, 1994).

Davis,S. & Davidson,B. *2020 Vision* (NY: Simon & Schuster, 1991).

Day,G.S. *Market Driven Strategy* (NY: Free Press, 1990).

Despande,R., & Webster,F.E. *Culture* (Cambridge: Marketing Sc. Inst., 1987).

Drucker,P. *Innovation & Entrepreneurship* (NY: Harper, 1985).

Drucker,P. *Post-Capitalist Society* (NY: Harper/Collins, 1993).

Feigenbaum,E. *Rise of the Expert Company* (NY: Vintage, 1988).

Gollub,J. *The Decade Matrix* (Reading, Mass: Addison-Wesley, 1993).

Handy,C. *The Age of Unreason* (Cambridge: Harvard U.Press, 1990).

Heldman,R.K. *Global Telecommunications* (NY: McGraw-Hill, 1992).

Itami,H. *Mobilizing Invisible Assets* (Cambridge: Harvard U.Press, 1987).

Jacobson,G. *Xerox: American Samurai* (N.Y.: Macmillan, 1986).

Johansen,R. *Leading Business Teams* (Reading: Addison-Wesley, 1991).

Johnson,H. *The Corporate Dream* (N.Y.: Carol, 1990).

Katzenbach,J.R. & Smith,D.K. *Wisdom of Teams* (Cambridge: Harvard UP, 1992).

Kearns,D. & Nadler,D. *How Xerox Reinvented Itself* (NY: Harper Business, 1992).

Keen,P. *Shaping the Future* (Cambridge: Harvard U.Press, 1991).

Klancy,K.J. & Shulman,R.S. *The Marketing Revolution* (NY: HarperBusiness, 1991).

Kotkin,J. *Tribes* (NY: Random House, 1993).

Kotler,P. & Turner,R.E. *Marketing Management* (Englewood: Prentice Hall, 1989).

Lazarus,G. *Marketing Immunity* (NY: Dow Jones, 1988).

Levitt,T. *Marketing Imagination* (NY: Free Press, 1983).

March,R.M. *Honoring the Customer* (NY: Wiley, 1990).

Masuda,Y. *Information Society* (Bethesda: World Future Society, 1981).

McCracken,G. *Culture & Consumption* (Indianapolis: Indiana U.P., 1990).

McKenna,R. *Relationship Marketing* (Reading: Addison-Wesley, 1991)

McKinnon,S.M. & Burns,W.J. *Information Mosaic* (Cambridge: Harvard UP, 1992).

McLuhan,M. *Understanding Media* (NY: McGraw-Hill, 1964).

Moriarty,R.T. *Managing Hybrid Channels* (Cambridge: Marketing Sc. Inst., 1988).

Morita,A. *Made in Japan: Akio Morita & Sony* (NY: Dutton, 1986).

Morton,M.S.S. *Corporation of the 1990s* (NY: Oxford U.Press, 1991).

Mowen,J.C. *Consumer Behavior* (NY: Macmillan, 1987).

Naisbitt,J. & Aburdene, P. *Megatrends 2000* (NY: Wm Morrow, 1990).

Ohmae,K. *Borderless World* (NY: Harper Business, 1990).

Ottman, Jacquelyn, *Green Marketing* (Lincolnwood, IL: NTC Publishing, 1993).

Parker,M.M. & Benson,R.J. *Info Economics* (Englewood: Prentice Hall, 1988).

Pattison,J.E. *Acquiring the Future* (Homewood: Irwin, 1990).

Peppers,D., & Rogers,M., *The One to One Future* (NY: Doubleday, 1993).

Peter,J.P. & Olson,J.C. *Consumer Behavior* (Homewood: Irwin, 1987).

Peters,T. *Thriving on Chaos* (NY: Knopf, 1987).

Peters,T. *Liberation Management* (NY: Knopf, 1992).

Peterson,R.A. *Future of U.S. Retailing* (NY: Quorum Books, 1992).

Pine,J. *Mass Customization* (Boston, Mass: Harvard UP, 1993).

Porter,M.E. *Competition in Global Industries* (Cambridge: Harvard UP, 1986).

Prahalad,C.K. & Doz,Y.L. *Multinational Mission* (NY: Free Press, 1987).

Rapp,S. & Collins,T. *Maximarketing* (NY: McGraw-Hill, 1987).

Rapp,S. & Collins,T. *Great Marketing Turnaround* (Englewood: Prentice, 1990).

Rheingold,H. *Virtual Reality* (NY: Simon & Schuster, 1991).

Roberts,M.L. & Berger,P.D. *Direct Marketing* (Englewood: Prentice Hall, 1989).

Rosenbluth,H.F. *Customer Comes Second* (NY: Morrow, 1992).

Rossiter,J.R. & Percy,L. *Advertising & Promotion* (NY: McGraw-Hill, 1987).

Sakaiya,T. *Knowledge Revolution* (Tokyo: Kodansha, 1991).

Savage,C. *Fifth Generation Management* (Bedford: Digital, 1992).

Senge,P.M. *The Fifth Discipline* (NY: Doubleday, 1990).

Snider,J. & Ziporyn,T. *Future Shop* (NY: St.Martin's Press, 1992).

Stalk,G. & Hout,T.M. *Competing Against Time* (NY: Free Press, 1990).

Strangelove,M. *How to Advertise on Internet* (Ottawa: Internet Business Jrnl, 1993).

Sveiby,K.E. & Lloyd,T. *Managing Knowhow* (London: Bloomsbury, 1987).

Tedlow,R.S. *New & Improved* (NY: Basic Books, 1990).

Terplan,K. *Communication Networks Management* (Englewood: Prentice, 1987).

Timpe,A. *Marketing* (NY: Facts on File, 1989).

Umano,S. *Law of Techno-Civilization* (Tokyo: Kodansha, 1984).

Vincent,D.R. *Information-Based Corporation* (Homewood: Irwin, 1990).

Weitzen,H.S. *Hypergrowth* (NY: Wiley, 1991).

Wendt,Henry, *Global Embrace* (NY: Harper Business, 1993).

Womack,J.P. *Machine That Changed The World* (NY: Macmillan, 1990).

Xerox Corp., *Guide to Waste Reduction & Recycling* (El Segundo, CA: Xerox, 1993).

Yip,G.S. *Total Global Strategy* (Englewood: Prentice, 1992).

Yoshino,M.Y. *Japanese Marketing System* (Cambridge: MIT Press, 1981).

Zemke,Ron. *The Service Edge* (NY: Penguin, 1990).

Index

For ease of reference, the Index is divided into six sections:

Companies/Organizations

ABC Television, 46

Advanced Battery Consortium, 87

Advanced Promotion Tech., 136

Airline Computer Tickets, 131

Albertson's, 136

Allstate Insurance, 20

Alpac, 103

Alpha Romeo, 154

AMD, 109

American Airlines, 10, 80, 131, 143

American Bankers' Association, 69, 131

American Cyanamid, 81, 88, 127

American Express, 41, 123

American Forestry Assn., 161

American Greetings, 20

American Stores, 136

Ameritech, 42, 51

Amway, 127-8

Anheuser-Busch, 134

Anixter, 100

Apple Computer, 9-10, 11, 16, 18, 19, 42, 46, 109

Asahi Glass, 110

Asia Pacific Economic Coop.(APEC), 50

AT&T, 10, 11, 12, 18, 28, 42, 45, 46, 87, 97, 107, 109, 132, 142, 160

Atlas Track & Tennis, 134

AutoData Marketing, 130

Automatic Coupon, 131

Auto Source, 159

Aveda, 134

Avon, 127-8

Bally's, 131, 142

Banc One, 79-80

Bankers Trust, 104

Barnes & Noble, 127

Bata Shoe, 105-6

L.L.Bean, 18-9

Bell Atlantic, 41-2, 129, 141

Ben & Jerry's, 20, 28, 113, 161

Benetton, 22, 28, 157

Bic, 122

BICC Cables, 75, 99

Big Cheese Pizza, 71

Binney & Smith, 98

Block (*see* H&R Block)

Body Shop (*see* The Body Shop)

Boeing, 10-1, 28, 75, 80, 83, 98, 154

Bon Appetit, 160

Brady's, 20, 159

Bruno's, 136

Business Council for Sustainable Development, 90

Cablevision Systems, 46

Campbell Soup, 57, 81, 118, 137

Canada Post, 44

Canadian Tire, 159

Canon, 75, 85, 149

Casio, 10

Catalina Marketing, 136

Century 21 Realty, 79

Brand/Trade Names

THE FUTURE:
What it will be like; what it all means.

An exciting public speaker and seminar presenter, Frank Feather delivers a solid message that truly connects:

> *A cogency and a clarity unsurpassed by any*
> *presentation on the future I've ever heard.*

—John M. Cranor III, President/CEO, **KFC International**

Frank's personally customized "future talks" are visionary, insightful, thought-provoking, pragmatic — and powerfully presented — with solid take-home benefits for your delegates.

You Decide the Content, Frank Delivers

He delivers what people expect in the 1990s: fresh, substantive ideas that matter in today's world. Each presentation — from title to content — is developed with your input to meet your event's specific goals.

Ever an optimist, he excites audiences with the prospects of dramatic social, technical, economic, and political change. Ever a pragmatist, he then draws out the no-nonsense meaning of these trends for your group.

And he's sensitive to audience dynamics. In 1980, Frank chaired the *1st Global Conference on the Future*, still the largest convention of its kind ever held, with 400 program sessions and 1,000 speakers.

Since then, he's made 700 of his own presentations to a raft of business, government, and association clients.

Exclusive with The Leigh Bureau

Frank Feather is exclusively represented worldwide by the Leigh Bureau. For a custom-tailored presentation on *The Future Consumer* or any other "future" topic, please contact one of the following agents.

- Ron Szymanski
- Tom Neilssen
- Robin Wolfson
- Fern Webber
- Danny Stern
- Les Tuerk
- Larry Leson

Phone: (908) 253-8600   Fax: (908) 253-8601
50 Division Street, Suite 200, Somerville, NJ 08876-2955